GW00372975

The Secrets of Speed Reading

Although this book reveals how at least one human reads at the rate of 25,000 words a minute, the purpose of *The Secrets of Speed Reading* is to show, in a fascinating sequence of instructions, exercises and self-tests, how almost anybody can reach reading speeds double, almost triple their present speeds, while also improving comprehension and enhancing enjoyment of the reading experience.

The **One Hour Wordpower** *series*

WORD BANK
Expanding Your Vocabulary
WORD CHECK
Using Words Correctly
GOOD GRAMMAR IN ONE HOUR
THE NAME BOOK
THE SECRETS OF SPEED READING
GUIDE TO WORDPLAY AND WORD GAMES
CRISP CLEAR WRITING IN ONE HOUR
SPELL CHECK
1000 Most Misspelled Words

One Hour Wordpower

The Secrets of
Speed Reading

GRAHAM KING

Mandarin
in association with
The Sunday Times

A Mandarin Paperback
THE SECRETS OF SPEED READING

First published in Great Britain 1993
by Mandarin Paperbacks
an imprint of Reed Consumer Books Ltd
Michelin House, 81 Fulham Road, London SW3 6RB
and Auckland, Melbourne, Singapore and Toronto

A CIP catalogue for this title
is available from the British Library
ISBN 0 7493 1523 7

Printed and bound in Great Britain
by Cox & Wyman Ltd, Reading, Berks

Contents

Acknowledgements

The publishers are grateful to *The Sunday Times* for permission to reproduce the extracts which appear on pages 57, 58 and 75:

'Thanks a Pillion' from an article by Jo Foley, published in *The Sunday Times* 1992

'Olive Oil Harvest' from an article by Mark Wallington, published in *The Sunday Times* 1992

Review of *The Secret History* by Penny Perrick, published in *The Sunday Times* 1992

Introduction

The days of the legendary leisure read have long gone.
Today, although we're reading more, we're forced to
accomplish it in less time – crammed somewhere in
between working and eating and driving and countless
other activities including four hours of television a day
(seven in the US).

Whether our reading is limited to newspapers,
magazines and the occasional novel, expanded by study
and training courses, or driven by a natural hunger for
information or literary enjoyment, the need to read and
understand faster has never been greater.

You appear to think so. After all, you've bought this
book because you want to know about speed reading.

A lot of rubbish has been written about what is
basically a fairly straightforward skill. Almost anyone
can learn to read faster; in many cases, spectacularly
faster. Most people can at the same time improve their
powers of concentration and level of comprehension.
To achieve this requires a certain determination,
diligence, practice – and instruction. That's what this
book provides.

The course of instruction in *The Secrets of Speed
Reading* is the collective result of observation and
experience over almost twenty years. In the process
hundreds of speed reading students were interviewed
and their reading performances assessed. Short-term
and long-term results were studied and laboratory
findings on eye movements and memory training were
analysed. Many teachers and instructors also
contributed valuable data on various training methods
in the UK and the US. And, finally, the techniques
cited in this book were themselves subjected to much
practical testing. Everything possible has been done to
design a course that can claim to be the most practical,
most comprehensive, most accessible and the one most
likely to produce better results than any other.

Whether your present reading speed is a lower-end 200 w.p.m. (words per minute), around the average 250 w.p.m. or a fast-paced 350 w.p.m., you have nothing to lose and everything to gain by following the course of instruction and exercises in this book.

You've taken the vital first step. Welcome to the world of reading efficiency!

The Secrets of Speed Reading

Some case histories

The world's fastest reader is an American, Howard Stephen Berg, clocked by the *Guinness Book of Records* at 25,000 words a minute. To prove his endurance over long texts, Berg gave a demonstration on a Cleveland TV show in which he read a 1,180-page non-fiction book (longer than *Gone With The Wind*) in under 20 minutes, or roughly a page a second. Unsurprisingly, in Berg's own speed reading course, he offers special instruction on how to turn pages efficiently.

Berg's achievement flies in the face of scientific evidence that the human eye simply cannot recognise words at that speed, let alone comprehend their meaning. And the truth is that Berg does not *read* texts in the accepted sense. What he has trained himself to do is to grab mentally at great speed what his mind senses to be the key elements of a text, so that he is able to give some account of what he has read, perhaps even answer questions about its content, but that is about all.

Like the man who earns a good living by his ability to recognise a classical music composition by merely looking at the grooves on an LP record, Berg is a speed reading freak, and his methods, although they continue to attract considerable numbers of starry-eyed devotees, have little application in the wider world. So let us descend from the stratosphere and examine the more meaningful achievements claimed for various rapid reading techniques.

One of the longest-established courses in the US is the 'Wade E. Cutler Accelerated Method' which claims that, since the 1960s, it has helped tens of thousands of students increase their reading speeds by 300%, along with an average improvement in comprehension of 13%.

Another widely promoted American course is the 'Evelyn Wood Speed Reading and Learning Program' which encourages its students to 'soar': that is, to read faster than the rate regarded as the sound barrier of speed reading – around 800–900 words per minute. Its principal quotes the case of Richard, a high school senior, who joined the course at a reading level of just under 300 w.p.m. Halfway through the three-week course Richard was clocking 1,000 w.p.m. and by the end was reading at 3,000 w.p.m. with 90% comprehension.

Another Evelyn Wood star pupil was Max, who began the course with a reading rate of 300 w.p.m. and a comprehension level of 48%. Three weeks later he graduated with a reading speed of 2,927 w.p.m. and a comprehension level of 92%. Such case histories are quoted for obvious reasons; what we don't learn about the Evelyn Wood method are the across-the-board results attained by the hundreds of thousands of people who have taken the course over the years.

In Britain the claims for speed reading are modest by comparison, although perhaps more credible. A survey of some of the courses supervised by various university departments indicates that doubling reading speed in a short time is an achievable target. These are the average results for four supervised courses:

Course	Increase in reading speed	Increase in comprehension
10 weeks	+110%	+19%
8 lessons	+100%	No change
1 week	+ 50%	Not known
1 week	+100%	Not known

More precise results are reported by the efficient reading specialists Manya and Eric De Leeuw, who have initiated a number of training courses in London. People attending their courses have attained an average increase in reading speed of 60% and an improvement in comprehension of around 10%.

While this may appear to be an unduly modest achievement, certain groups positively romped ahead. The De Leeuws found that medium-fast readers (300–350 w.p.m.) could expect the greatest gains, and quote the case history of a group of ten psychiatrists who began a course with an average speed of 334 w.p.m. and a comprehension level of 78%, and finished it with an average reading speed of 647 w.p.m. and a comprehension level of 85%.

Leaving aside the supersonic results claimed by some courses it is clear that quite substantial improvement in reading efficiency and understanding are within the grasp of almost everyone. Doubling and even tripling reading speed without loss of comprehension is, on ample evidence, a good possibility for most people.

And this certainly includes you.

Self check: How fast do you read?

So far, you have merely been *reading* this book. From this point, however, you are going to be *involved* with it. There is no point in reading on unless you are prepared to contribute some effort – not a lot, so don't be alarmed – towards improving your reading efficiency.

Our first task is to determine your status as a reader – your present reading speed and approximate level of comprehension. Three short and simple tests will give us a fairly good measure of your skills: all you are asked to do is to read the following three texts at your normal speed – the pace, for example, that you'd read a magazine article that interested you.

For this and other exercises in this book, and for daily practice, you will need a stopwatch or a watch or clock with a second sweep hand: seconds count! You'd also be wise to attempt the tests and exercises in a comfortable, interruption-free environment.

Self Check Reading Test No.1

For this test, make a note of where the second hand is when you begin so that you can stop after exactly 60 seconds have elapsed. Make sure you understand what you're reading, too; there's a follow-up quiz to see if you've been paying attention.

START

1 Modern Madagascar seems little changed from the Madagas-
2 car of 150 years ago; the tales of 19th-century and
3 modern travellers are remarkably similar. Politically,
4 the country is as rickety and as unpredictable as its
5 railways, and it remains one of the poorest in the world.
6 Culturally, wide-eyed innocence still prevails alongside
7 tolerated villainy, although the population is becoming
8 more francophile and more Catholic. To most Europeans it
9 is about as unknown as Outer Mongolia and today even less

10 accessible than Albania; and the only Malagasay who seems
11 to have made any impact on the world's stage was
12 Andreamentene Razafinkeriepo, perhaps better known as
13 Andy Rasaf, who wrote a lot of songs for the jazz pianist
14 Fats Waller.
15   Ecologically, virtually nothing has changed. If you
16 look at a map of Africa you will readily see where, some
17 200 million years ago, the great chunk that is now Mada-
18 gascar broke off and drifted eastwards. Since then, the
19 island, and the flora and fauna that travelled with it,
20 evolved separately, so that this massive ark – a thous-
21 and miles long and nearly three times the size of the
22 British Isles – today contains a spectacular wealth of
23 indigenous species, including over ten thousand plants,
24 of which three-quarters are peculiar to Madagascar; over
25 200 butterflies, 140 frogs, and half the world's cham-
26 eleons. Unique species abound, from liverworts to
27 lemurs; there are 30 of the latter, including one of the
28 biggest attractions, the screaming indri lemur, and the
29 even more curious aye-aye, a four-handed nocturnal lemur
30 the size of a cat and somewhere between a rodent and a
31 monkey. This animal has a grossly attenuated claw grow-
32 ing from one of its middle fingers expressly designed to
33 capture its favourite food, a succulent wood-boring larva
34 which retreats to the far end of its long tunnel when
35 disturbed. But at the beginning of the 19th century,
36 before the arrival of a succession of British missionary
37 naturalists, almost nothing was known about these wonders.
38   Today, sadly, the time-warped natural wonderland
39 studied by those earnest missionaries a century and a half
40 ago is now in such mortal danger that it is designated a
41 top priority conservation crisis. Much of the island is
42 surrounded by a sea of brick-red liquid mud several miles
43 wide, the product of probably the worst erosion in the
44 world today. In just 25 years the population has doubled;
45 the forests have been destroyed wholesale for farms and
46 fuel. Smuggling rare species is rife and the aye-aye is
47 now probably the world's rarest mammal. On its present
48 course, Madagascar will be totally unrecognisable in less
49 than half a century; all that was unique will be found
50 only in museums and natural history books.

                                             STOP

Estimating your speed. Make a note of the numbered line where you stopped after exactly 60 seconds. Add a nought and that will give you your reading speed in words per minute. Thus if you stopped at line 29, your speed for this test is approximately 290 w.p.m.

Estimating your level of comprehension. So much for speed – but have you understood all you have read? To get some idea of how much information you absorbed from the test text, tick YES/NO to the following questions (without, of course, referring back to the text!):

Comprehension Test No. 1

	YES	NO
1. Madagascar is less accessible than Mongolia	——	——
2. It is one of the world's poorest countries	——	——
3. It broke off from Africa 20 million years ago	——	——
4. Half the world's lemur species live there	——	——
5. The population speaks mainly Portuguese	——	——
6. The human population has tripled in 25 years	——	——
7. The favourite food of the aye-aye is frogs	——	——
8. Madagascar is 1,000 miles long	——	——
9. It is also about three times the size of the British Isles	——	——
10. One of its unique species is the indri chameleon	——	——

Check the answers on page 107. By adding a nought to your score you will arrive at your approximate comprehension level, in percentage terms, for this test. Enter both scores in the box below for later comparison.

Reading speed	Level of comprehension
w.p.m.	%

Such a simplistic test can only provide a rough indicator of your reading skills, but we can get a more accurate reading from the results of a couple more tests, slightly different in style although no more difficult than the first test. Here is No.2, to be read at your normal reading speed.

Self Check Reading Test No.2

Make a note of the *exact* time you start:

min	sec

START

Literature Can Be Dangerous To Your Health

In 1981 a New Orleans writer named Edward R. Grant III was hauled before the Federal Court and given a five-year suspended sentence for causing a public mischief. He was also ordered to pay $24,000 costs to the Coast Guard, the amount it claimed it had spent looking for him. Mr Grant had abandoned his car on a causeway, leaving a note that implied he had jumped off and drowned. The incident sparked off a state-wide hunt for his body which was eventually found, alive and well.

What had prompted Mr Grant to take this action was the failure of his book, *Saints in the Shadows*, which, after a great deal of difficulty, had found a publisher only to be rejected by the public. It had not only failed to attract a single critical notice, but no trace of any sale could be discovered either. In desperation, the author decided to create a 'media event' by faking suicide – inspired by the real suicide of the Pulitzer Prize-winning novelist John Kennedy Toole twelve years before.

The Toole suicide is a much-thumbed chapter in American literary mythology. There are, of course, other famous literary suicides, the tragic results of despair, madness and personal catastrophe, but if there is to be a patron saint of rejection, it has to be John Kennedy Toole. The case for his canonisation gains further force from the cause of his self-immolation, *A Confederacy of Dunces*, which, rescued from almost certain oblivion, was posthumously published and immediately recognised as a modern literary masterpiece.

Toole died unpublished in 1969 at the age of 32, mourned by his admiring mother, Thelma, with whom the lonely young man had had an unusually close relationship. Mrs Toole was convinced of her son's genius and in an extended act of faith spent years battering at the publishers' doors in a vain attempt to have the novel published.

It was not until 1976, seven years after her son's death, that she at last beheld a ray of hope. She had telephoned a New Orleans English lecturer, Walker Percy, with the request that he read the novel. Percy remembers the occasion clearly:

'Why would I want to do that?' he asked her.

'Because it is a great novel,' she said.

Like most in his profession, Percy had developed plenty of ploys to avoid this sort of chore, and the last thing he needed was the manuscript-toting mother of a dead novelist. But Mrs Toole was persistent and the next day Walker Percy was contemplating a pile of smudgy, barely readable typescript. 'There was no getting out of it,' he later wrote. 'Only one hope remained – that I could read a few pages and that they would be bad enough for me, in good conscience, to read no further. Usually I can do just that. Indeed the first paragraph often suffices. My only fear was that this one might not be bad enough, or might be just good enough, so that I would have to keep reading.

'In this case I read on. And on. First with the sinking feeling that it was not bad enough to quit, then with a prickle of interest, then a growing excitement, and finally an incredulity; surely it was not possible that it was so good.'

A Confederacy of Dunces is a rumbustious tragicomedy centred on Ignatious J. Rielly, a flatulent slob and loquacious genius who's a mix of a half-mad Oliver Hardy, a corpulent Don Quixote and a perverse Thomas Aquinas. Percy was so entranced by the novel that, after some excerpts were printed in the *New Orleans Review* in 1978, he helped guide it to Grove Press in New York, where it was published in 1980. It was launched to a pandemonium of praise. The *New York Times* judged it to be 'a masterwork of comedy' while *Publishers Weekly* thought 'there is a touch of genius about Toole and what he has created'. It very quickly became a modern classic: 'One might have to travel as far back as Swift to find so cutting a work of humour. No doubt about it, this book is destined to become a classic', confirmed the *Baltimore Sun*. It was awarded the Pulitzer Prize in 1981.

There is, in the John Kennedy Toole story, an ironic postscript. Among his papers existed the manuscript of a novel he had written when barely 16, and which had been entered in an almost forgotten literary competition. The novel was called *The Neon Bible*. Set in the bigoted southern American 'Bible belt', it has obvious autobiographical links with the author, who is cast as a lonely, mother-loving misfit, touchingly observing his family and the Mississippi small-town community struggling with their economic and emotional poverty. With the kind of brazen harlotry for which the publishing trade is noted, this often brilliant but nevertheless immature work was gleefully disinterred and published, against the protests of Toole's ageing mother and after a bitter battle through the courts – twenty years after its author, his masterpiece having been rejected by at least eight publishers, pushed a hose into the exhaust pipe of his car and gassed himself.

STOP

Record the exact time you finished reading:

min	sec

To find your reading speed for this test, simply refer to the w.p.m. table on page 109.

Comprehension Test No. 2

		YES	NO
1.	The name of the author who committed suicide was John Kennedy O'Toole	___	___
2.	He died in 1979	___	___
3.	His mother's name was Thelma	___	___
4.	The famous book he wrote was *A Confederacy of Dunces*	___	___
5.	It was published ten years after his death	___	___
6.	It won a Pulitzer Prize	___	___
7.	The New Orleans English lecturer who helped get it published was Percy Walker	___	___

8. The typescript was barely legible   ____   ____
9. Another novel, *The Neon Bible*,
   was published just before he died   ____   ____
10. This novel was set in New Orleans   ____   ____

Check the answers on page 107, add a nought to your score (the number of correct answers out of ten) and enter your comprehension level for this test, together with your reading speed, in the box:

Reading speed	Level of comprehension
w.p.m.	%

Later on, as you proceed through the exercises and benefit from some practice, you will be anxious to find out whether or not your speed and understanding are improving and to what extent. For this reason it is important to get as accurate a fix as possible on your present reading ability. This is why you are asked to attempt this short final test.

Self Check Reading Test No. 3

Read this at your normal reading speed. But first make a note of your exact starting time:

min	sec

START

In the Bay of Naples there exist two creatures, a medusa and a sea slug, whose lives are so inseparable that they have in almost every respect become one.

They are parasitical upon each other. Separately, they could not exist. Together, their combined histories form a perfect circle, with no beginning and no end. Even more paradoxically, they reproduce separately.

It is therefore difficult to know where to begin, but we might break the circle at a point where the jellyfish exists as a tiny parasite attached to the slug. The jellyfish produces offspring which grow into large, strikingly beautiful medusae.

The slug also produces larvae, which drift upwards through the water to become trapped within the food-hunting tentacles of the medusa. But instead of being digested by the jellyfish the larvae turn from potential prey to predator, and begin to eat their host.

As the slugs eat, they grow to full size, while the medusa disappears, bit by bit, until only a tiny piece of the original organism remains. This, as you may have guessed, attaches itself to the ventral surface of one of the slugs, which is precisely the point at which we broke the circle.

STOP

Note down the exact time you finished reading, refer to the w.p.m. table on page 109 for your reading speed, and then proceed to the comprehension text without any further reference to the text.

Comprehension Test No. 3

1. The life cycles of the medusa and the sea slug are enacted in the warm waters of the _____

2. Both creatures are classed as _____

3. Do the (a) young slugs eat the jellyfish, or (b) do the adult jellyfish digest the slug larvae?

4. Do they (a) reproduce with each other, or (b) separately?

5. During their life cycles, is (a) the medusa host to the sea slug; (b) is the sea slug host to the jellyfish, or (c) are they both host and parasite to each other?

Check the answers on page 107, multiply your score out of five by 20 (ie 3 correct × 20 = 60%) and record the results in the panel:

Reading speed	Level of comprehension
w.p.m.	%

To complete this self-test, average your three results by adding them up and dividing by three. For example:

Test 1	290 w.p.m.	70% comprehension
Test 2	260 w.p.m.	60% comprehension
Test 3	270 w.p.m.	80% comprehension
Total	820	210
Average (divide by 3)	273 w.p.m.	70% comprehension

Following that formula, record your own present reading speed and comprehension in the box for future reference:

Date	Average reading speed	Average level of comprehension
	w.p.m.	%

Reading speeds vary enormously. It is reckoned, however, that the normal (that is, untrained) reading speed of an average intelligent adult will fall somewhere between 200–300 w.p.m., and most likely between 225–250 w.p.m., with a 50–60% comprehension level.

If your speed for these three tests is below 200 w.p.m., don't despair; there are remedial aspects to this course which should have you reading much faster in no time. And if you've clocked your speed at considerably more than 300 w.p.m., don't throw the book away either; there is sound evidence that those with a normal reading speed of 300–350 w.p.m. provide the finest raw material for super-fast reading with near 100% comprehension.

The next chapter will give you a more complete picture of reading speeds and comprehension levels, and what they mean.

Reading speeds and comprehension levels

Surprisingly, very few adults were ever taught how to read quickly and efficiently, and in fact within the education system little attention is paid to this important activity. A student given an overnight assignment to read a 5,000 word text is asked simply that it be read and understood, with no enquiry next day as to how long it took. While one student might polish it off in half an hour, another might struggle all evening; and the slow reader, lacking advice or comparison, might never realise that he or she is, in fact, a slow reader. Such a student may well be bright and intelligent, but without instruction will be disadvantaged, possibly for a lifetime.

Pressures and pleasures sometimes come to the rescue. The pressures involved in slogging through schoolwork, course work, training programmes and technical texts can certainly push our natural w.p.m. rates up a notch or two. And the pleasures of ripping through a clutch of novels during a holiday can actually introduce us, unconsciously, to a form of speed reading. But we are never likely to realise our full potential without some instruction in the techniques of improved reading efficiency.

The simple fact is that there is no reason why a snail's-pace reader should remain in the slow lane. Nor is there any need for the majority of us to try to attain speeds in excess of, say, 400 or 500 w.p.m. For most of us the middle lane will do very nicely, with the ability to swing out when the occasion demands. There is probably an optimum reading speed for everyone, according to a person's needs and abilities.

So what, exactly, is the speed spectrum? Here is a table, compiled from a great number of diverse sources, that will give you some idea of where you fit now, and where you might eventually find yourself. It assumes, by the way, a comprehension level of 60–70%:

Speed w.p.m.	
125–160	Average speaking speed
150	Speed for a difficult text; otherwise slow
175	Lower end of average; average 14-year-old secondary school students
200	Just below average
225	Average intelligent American adult
250	Average UK adult
275	Above average
300	Probably in the upper 20%; first-year undergraduate; upper end of average
350	Medium to fast reader; reading speed of many teachers and professionals
400	Fast
500	At this speed you can read a 60,000 word book or novel in two hours
600	Very fast; experienced professional readers
700	Professional book reviewers
800	'Subsonic'
900	'Supersonic'
1000	Phenomenal

So where do you fit in? Before you jump to any conclusions, check the following table which, although it was drawn up over 30 years ago, is still one of the best documented records of reading speeds. In the study, under the aegis of the Department of Scientific and Industrial Research, the reading abilities of 147 people were measured. These people were undertaking polytechnic courses; 82 were from business groups, while the remaining 65 were from general classes. The following table records their initial or normal reading speeds:

Words per minute	Number of readers	Percentage
Under 200	15	10.2%
200–239	51	34.7%
240–269	28	19.0%
270–299	22	15.0%
300–319	12	8.1%
320–359	12	8.1%
360–399	6	4.2%
Above 400	1	0.7%

You will see that 45% of the sample had a normal reading speed of under 240 w.p.m., and only one in five achieved speeds of 300 w.p.m. or more.

The purpose of familiarising you with these comparative speeds is twofold:

- As with just about every other ability, it is useful to know where you stand in the pecking order
- More positively, you can now begin to fix on an attainable target

For example, if the three self-check tests revealed that your reading rate is 220 w.p.m., even the most modest improvement of 50 w.p.m. will propel you into the top 35%! Increase your reading rate by 100 w.p.m. and you're in the top 20%. And if you double your present speed of 220 w.p.m. you're in the elite company of the fast reader. All of this is possible with practice.

Beyond 400 w.p.m. is specialist territory, the preserve of people, usually professionals, who have to soak up large quantities of print: publisher's readers, book reviewers, journalists, scientists, politicians, executives and so on. It is not unusual for such fast readers to achieve over 600 w.p.m. in bursts, which means that whole books can be opened, read and shut at a single short sitting. There may be no reason why you shouldn't manage these speeds either.

Some experts maintain that conventional speed reading reaches its limit at around 700–800 w.p.m. when it is necessary to pass through something like a sound barrier. Speeds below 800–900 w.p.m. are, they say, 'subsonic' or 'sub-vocal'; above that you soar into the stratosphere where pages flip by every four or five seconds and the act of reading becomes a near-mystical sensation. If you have aspirations to become a Concorde of speed reading, there is more on this phenomenon in a later chapter.

But for those of us destined to fly just above or below the clouds, understanding the text we're reading is as important as speed: speed is pointless without comprehension.

It is a common belief that to read slowly is to comprehend thoroughly, and that to read fast is to miss things and thus misunderstand. This simply isn't true, and it could be said that the reverse is more often the case. Sufficient research has been done to suggest that the slow reader, ponderously hesitating on details, is the one more likely to miss the point of a text, while the fast reader, alive and alert and with adrenalin running, is in a better frame of mind not only to grasp the essentials, but to appreciate other qualities of the writing besides.

Another half-truth about reading is that you will read a text faster if it interests you, and slower if you're bored by the subject. While no conclusive research exists to prove this one way or another, there is evidence suggesting that when you are reading about something you enjoy – gardening, cookery, horse racing, boating – you are just as inclined to dwell lovingly on all the details as to race breathlessly through it.

What has been established, however, is that reading speed and comprehension are directly linked to concentration. We are all aware of those occasions when something on our minds, some worry or distraction, forces us to re-read and re-digest; often, several pages will flip by when we will suddenly realise that we haven't really read, understood or remembered a single thing. If we are determined to improve our reading efficiency we must, with an effort of conscious willpower, tackle the problem of defective concentration.

A person's level of comprehension is far more difficult to determine than reading speed, and not too much importance should be attached to the score achieved for a single test. The only way to arrive at a reasonably reliable figure is to average the results of several tests. So far, the information you have about your comprehension level is based on the average of three short tests but at best this will only be an approximation with a 10% margin of error either way.

If, in these tests, your average comprehension level fell between 40–60%, then you are in the average band. Your own commonsense will tell you that this is too low; throwing away half of everything you read hardly makes sense. So you should set yourself a target: to improve your average comprehension level by at least 10%, even 20%. This book will help you achieve it. The next two chapters include comprehension tests, so that by incorporating the results from these with your previous scores, you should have a somewhat more accurate picture of your powers of assimilation.

Preparation 1: The role of the eye

The process of reading involves

- Eye movement
- Character recognition
- Assimilation and understanding
- Remembering and recall

In this chapter we will be discussing the first two aspects of reading, both of which concern your eyesight.

Your eyes see only when they are still. If you turn your head suddenly from one side of a room to the other you will record images at the start and finish but only a blur in between. The nature of the printed word is that it is *still*, so therefore your eyes must be still every time you read a word or group of words. As you read along a printed line of words, your eyes will travel, stop, travel, stop, travel, stop – to the end of the line and then down to the next. Each of these movements takes only a fraction of a second, but those fractions are vital when it comes to reading efficiency.

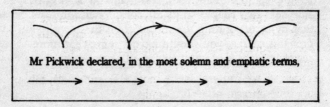

Mr Pickwick declared, in the most solemn and emphatic terms,

How the eye reads a line of print

Each time the eyes stop it is called a fixation, which is the period in which the reading matter is recognised, understood and stored into the memory.

But fixations are only a part of the reading equation. What is important to the reader is the *size* of the fixation – the size of the 'bite', as it were. Here are the fixation patterns of a slow reader, an average reader, and a fast reader:

1. Fixation pattern of a slow reader

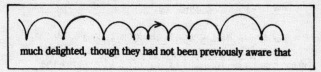

much delighted, though they had not been previously aware that

2. Fixation pattern of an average reader

Corinthian pillars, and a music gallery, and a Tompion clock,

3. Fixation pattern of a fast reader

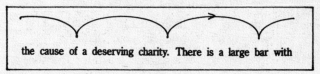

the cause of a deserving charity. There is a large bar with

You see the difference, don't you? The slow reader is reading the text word by single word, and you can see why this must be a snail-like process. The average reader, however, includes unimportant words with key words, requiring fewer fixations and fewer eye movements; thus the line is read faster. The fast reader, as we can see, is the most efficient of all, taking in whole phrases at a visual gulp.

That, in a nutshell, is the basis of reading efficiency.

Here is a sentence of 20 words that the average reader would read and understand in around three seconds with a fixation pattern which might look like this:

Snow at Christmas is all very well on cards
but it makes a long winter if it comes too soon.

A fast reader, on the other hand, would deal with the sentence in half that time by grouping more words:

<u>Snow at Christmas</u>   <u>is all very well on cards</u>
<u>but it makes</u>   <u>a long winter</u>   <u>if it comes too soon.</u>

The key to reading speed is the ability to recognise larger chunks of printed matter per fixation. This ability has to be built from the ground up and the foundation for it is quick and accurate character recognition.

In a single fixation an efficient reader might take in a phrase like *The storm was catastrophic*. But reaching that point has involved an evolutionary journey from single letters, *C-A-T*, to *cat*, and ultimately to *catastrophe*. Such a progression is determined, initially, by the eye's ability to see and the mind's capacity to respond to a symbol; this is called recognition, and it varies immensely from individual to individual. Try the following two tests to check your character recognition rate.

Character Recognition Test 1   Set your watch to time yourself for this test in which you are required to touch each letter in correct alphabetical order:

C	G	J	B
H	A	D	I
E	F	L	K
Time taken:		sec	

Character Recognition Test 2   Set your watch again; this time you are asked to touch the numbers in correct numerical order:

6	10	2	11
3	8	4	9
12	7	1	5
Time taken:			sec

If your time on either test was 8–9 seconds, then you have an average recognition rate. If you took less than seven seconds your reaction time is excellent, but if you spent ten seconds or more your reaction time is a bit on the tardy side.

Sluggish reaction times could result from several factors, from faulty eyesight to restricted visual span, and we must recognise also that everyone differs in their response levels which may change with circumstances and age. Not all car drivers are equal, as we know.

Unless there is some incurable organic problem standing in the way, most people can improve their character recognition rate by conscious effort, concentration and alertness. There is also a structured approach which involves expanding those fixations. And fundamental to this is an understanding of what visual span is all about.

On a printed page, the limit of vision for a normal person is an ellipse about 7cm or 3 inches wide. But that is the outer limit for character recognition; only a few words within this area may be read quickly and comfortably.

In other words, if the central area represents what you are reading now (i.e. recognising and understanding), the area of peripheral vision represents your potential. Widening your visual span by

ual absence of his two friends, which their my
ir during the whole morning had by no means to — Limit of vision
It was therefore, with more than ordinary
rose to greet them when they again entered; ;
in ordinary interest that he inquired what had
n them from his society. In reply to his q
point, Mr Snodgrass was about to offer a — Area of peripheral vi
of the circumstances just now detailed, when
checked by observing that there were present,
nan and their stage coach companion of the p
another stranger of equally singular appearance
orn looking man, whose sallow face and deeply — Focus point
ere rendered still more striking than nature h
y the straight black hair which hung in matted
down his face. His eyes were almost unnatural

recognising more words within this limit of vision is
one of the keys to efficient reading.

To highlight this point further, try these little tests.
The first of these is a simple line of numbers. Fix your
eye on the underlined number in the centre and then,
without moving your eyes, see how far you can read
in either direction:

7   5   0   3   9   2   <u>5</u>   6   7   2   0   3   5

With some concentration you should read out to the o
on either side, although the numbers may be a little
blurred. Some may even get the outer numbers within
their range of vision. But even if your in-focus vision
had reached its limit at the zeroes, it means that you
really do possess the ability to read a phrase like this
one at a single glance:

Reading phrases is efficient reading

What this demonstrates is that you are probably not
using your eyes' recognition capacity to their fullest
extent.

Here's another test. This time, fix your eye on the

centre line of letters and see if you can comfortably
recognise the letters on either side, line by line:

AN	K	VG
LF	Y	TD
WS	C	PH
GN	E	HJ
MI	S	JX

For people with one eye more near- or far-sighted
than the other, one of the outer rows may be blurred,
but most should be able to recognise all the letters
without too much trouble.

Curiously, the more complex patterns of words are
often memorable and thus easier to identify than single
characters. Try this test. Again, fix your eye on the
centre word and see if you can recognise the two words
either side on each line:

she went	are	told him
the eye	for	blue sky
he said	and	sad tale
a laugh	why	soft sand
red bird	she	low note

Can you read all five words in each line without moving
your eyes left or right? If you can, then you are capable,
with practice, of reading entire lines of an average
newspaper column in a single fixation.

Whether or not the eyes can be trained to increase
their eyespan is still under investigation. But that is
not the issue here; what has been proven is that the
potential of our *existing* visual span – limited and
imperfect though it may be – is invariably and often
woefully under-exploited.

We are now coming to grips with the part the eyes
play in the process of reading. Our eyes move, pause,
and recognise characters. This pause is called a **fixation**:
a visual 'bite'. The movements between fixations are

entirely non-productive. Therefore the less movement between fixations the better. The conclusion is that to read faster we need to increase the productivity of our fixations. We do this by tapping into the unused potential of our natural visual span.

A researcher at the Reading and Study Centre in New York reportedly found that the average American adult recognised only 1.06 words per fixation. This means that to read a single line of an average book the eye stopped between seven and eight times, and also made seven or eight unproductive trips between each fixation. Half the time spent reading each line was wasted.

To efficient reading instructors this amounts to a combination of laziness, ignorance and poor technique – all faults that are curable.

The process of reading begins with the eyes, and part of the preparations to improve reading efficiency should include their physical care. Eye defects that go uncorrected are unnecessary obstructions in the way of rapid reading and the enjoyment of it.

For many if not most of us, reading is an important, sometimes vital activity, so it is worth paying attention to a few details. People who take up golf or squash spend hundreds of pounds on equipment, clothing, coaching and facilities but resist investing a penny on the arguably more useful, necessary and enjoyable act of reading.

A good reading light and a reasonably intrusion-free environment should be considered essential. Posture is important, too, which may mean acquiring a comfortable chair you can call your own. Finally, if reading is to play a more prominent role in your life, you should practise the simple trick of pausing every minute or so and focusing on some distant object, through a window if there is one or in your mind if there isn't. This exercise reduces reading fatigue and helps to relax the eye muscles, and it certainly pays off in extended reading sessions – even at the expense of your w.p.m.!

Comprehension Test No.4

This test consists of questions on what you've just read.

		TRUE	FALSE
1.	The normal 'limit of vision' on a printed page is about 7cm or 3 inches	_____	_____
2.	A fast reader reads a line of print word by word	_____	_____
3.	Words are often easier to identify than single characters	_____	_____
4.	A fixation is the area within the eye's peripheral sphere of vision	_____	_____
5.	The character recognition rate is the speed at which you respond to a symbol	_____	_____
6.	One cause of slow character recognition is near-sightedness	_____	_____
7.	The eyes can be trained to double their visual span	_____	_____
8.	The key to efficient reading is to recognise larger 'bites' of text for each fixation	_____	_____
9.	The average US adult is reported to recognise 1.06 words per fixation	_____	_____
10.	The eye movements between fixations can be highly productive	_____	_____

Check the answers on page 107 and award yourself 10 percentage points for each correct question; thus if you score seven correct, your comprehension score for this test is 70%. Enter your score in the box below:

Test No.4	
Level of comprehension:	%

Preparation 2: The mind and the memory

The brain is the major organ of our nervous system that originates and controls all our emotions, thought and speech. Rather simplistically, the brain has right and left sides. In most people the right side controls the visual and imaginative elements – intuition, and visual and creative thinking – while the left side does the logical and analytical thinking. This includes our verbal aptitude for speaking and reading.

The mind, however, is not an organ but a system, an unfinished jigsaw with an infinite number of pieces, all of which relate in some way to each other. That is the important thing about the mind: it is a process through which its owner thinks by relating some new fact or experience to those already 'in storage'.

Which brings us to the memory. Again, the most brilliant surgeons cannot see or touch the memory and in fact they do not even know where in the brain it might be lurking. But we do know, or think we know, a few things about it.

There is, for a start, no single memory but a series of memories for specialised purposes. The capture of an item of information from a reading experience might begin as an entry into our sensory memory. This memory records momentary images like separate characters and forms them into words.

The resultant images then feed into our workaday or short-term memory which might hold the information for a second or two. A good example of its capability is that it will hold the numerals of a phone number just long enough for us to dial it.

Then, if the information is relevant to our needs, it is transferred to our long-term memory. This is an immense storage bin and because the information fed into it must be capable of being retrieved, it is stored by a coding system. We don't know a lot about this system but we can theorise that it probably works by association: all the information in there is related to something else – images, words, sounds, smells – to enable it to recognise the piece of information when we push the recall button.

Well, sometimes. You've experienced the feeling: you know that name or date or word is in there but you can't think of it right now! Hours later, perhaps, out it pops.

In very simple terms the three elements of memory are –

- RECORDING – comprehending and learning
- RETAINING – long-term storage
- RECALLING – retrieving on demand

Of these three elements it is believed that no training methods exist to improve the retention functions of the memory. There is, however, ample evidence that the recording function does respond to certain types of training.

Much of this work is done at memory clinics which were founded some years ago in the US and now exist in Britain. Memory training, understandably, is largely restricted to people suffering from memory impairment. The work is still to a great extent developmental and the best results have been obtained with the rehabilitation of young people with brain damage; tragically, very little improvement is recorded by the sufferers of Alzheimer's disease.

But for a normal person, what are the secrets of a good memory? We all know of freak memories; the pianist Claudio Arrau could retain in his memory the music for no less than 40 two-and-a-half hour concerts. Winston Churchill was reputed to have memorised Milton's *Paradise Lost* in a week and could certainly remember long speeches word for word after a single reading. Compared to these feats our own average memories seem shamefully inadequate.

There are a few facts we do know about enhancing the workings of the memory, but none of them will strike you as an amazing revelation.

The first and perhaps most important of these is that if you have the conscious intention of remembering something, you almost certainly will. With concentration, you can 'talk' the information into your memory. There will be times when you may not be able to recall it on demand, but it will be in there, somewhere.

It also helps if you understand the information, and are interested in it. This helps your memory relate the information to many other items in your storage tank, and we believe that the more relationships there are, the more effectively new information will be stored for retrieval.

The process of memorising by repetition can also work, as millions of schoolchildren of former generations can attest. The essence of this method is to reduce information to the bare essentials: thus an epic historical enterprise is boiled down to *Spain/Columbus/1492/America*. If you can recall that basic information, it is argued, the memory will be further stimulated and regurgitate the details.

Some readers of this book may be of the age when they begin to apologise for their memories on account of, well, age. Unless there is some organic or mental impairment the real reason for mental lapses is simply laziness. Lapses of memory are not confined to older people; the young have them too.

On the contrary, if we believe in the relationship theory there are good reasons why memories should *improve* with age. The more there is in there, the more there is for fresh information to relate to, and be retained. The same might be said about the process of recall – we know it's in there, but how do we get it out? Improving recall is largely a matter of determination; of requesting your memory for the information in various ways – by knocking on a number of doors. If you try hard enough, by thinking about words, names, events or experiences that might be associated with the elusive information, it should eventually present itself in the 'answer' drawer. Keeping a memory in top gear isn't a matter of magic; it requires exercise and effort.

Comprehension Test No. 5

This test consists of questions on the chapter you've just read.

	TRUE	FALSE
1. The mind is the major organ of the nervous system	____	____
2. Everyone possesses not one, but several memories	____	____
3. Information is stored in our memories by a coding or 'relationship' system	____	____
4. The recall or retrieval function of our memories can be easily trained	____	____
5. Churchill memorised a complete Shakespeare play in a week	____	____
6. Mental lapses have little to do with age	____	____

7. On a previous page, four essential facts were given about a certain epic historical journey. As a test of memory and recall, what were the four facts?

1 _____
2 _____
3 _____
4 _____

Check the answers on page 108 and award yourself 10 percentage points for each one correct. For Question 7, award 10 points for each of the four facts you get correct. Enter your score in the box below:

Now average the results of all five of the comprehension tests you've done so far:

YOUR AVERAGE OF COMPREHENSION TESTS 1, 2 and 3 (from box at end of Chapter 2)	_____%
+ SCORE FROM TEST No.4	_____%
+ SCORE FROM TEST No.5	_____%
TOTAL	_____%
DIVIDE BY 3 TO GET OVERALL AVERAGE	_____%

That average of five tests will represent a fair approximation of your level of comprehension. Let's improve it!

Speed reading techniques: A mixed bag

There have been so many claims made for various speed reading techniques over the years that it would not be unusual for anyone about to embark on a reading efficiency course to be bewildered and not a little unconvinced that any method could work. And many of the claims are as bizarre as the methods.

An enterprise undertaken without confidence is almost certain to fail. That is why, in this chapter, we will take time out to examine most of the rapid reading techniques and courses currently being offered around the world. The purpose is not to disparage them but to let you draw your own conclusions as to whether or not they might work for you.

No single method can ever claim to be infallible; nor can any particular technique *guarantee* an improvement in reading speed or comprehension. But being informed about the various methods will put you in a better position to make your own judgments about the techniques that are offered in this book. If you are to make any real progress improving your reading proficiency it is of primary importance that you have confidence in the instructor and the methods. It is to be hoped that you will have complete confidence in both.

Eye span and eye swing

Although existing research suggests that the eyes cannot be 'trained', many courses persist in forcing students to enlarge their span of vision and to practise rhythmical eye movements in the quest for greater speed.

As we saw in the chapter on the eyes, we are stuck with the eye span we were born with. It is possible, of course, that we are not using it efficiently or to full capacity, and in this regard some improvement might be achieved.

Another scientifically unsupported theory about the eyes is that they can be trained to move rhythmically. This is called 'eye swing' and the idea is to have the eyes swing like liquid silk from phrase to phrase and line to line. It sounds highly desirable, as the eyes of the average reader proceed on a saw-tooth path along a line, dwelling, hesitating and meandering through the course of a page: all alarmingly inefficient. But is it possible to practise this swing, like a golf swing, to achieve efficient, rhythmical eye movement? The evidence, or lack of it, suggests not.

A method in vogue a decade or so ago was called 'top of the line skimming'. This system called for its users not to enlarge their visual span but to restrict it: to train the eye to recognise just the top of each letter. The idea was for the eye to tear along the top of the line at great speed, which was attainable because the bottom two-thirds of each letter, each word and each line could be dispensed with. As implausible as it sounds, the method claimed many successful graduates.

With such a method, we have to teach our brain to believe what the eye sees. With 'top of the line skimming' the eye sees only part of a letter but the brain recognises the whole. This notion is stretched further by a technique called 'layered reading'. In this case the brain is asked to interpret whole slabs of text. Each page is mentally divided into a series of six, eight or ten rectangles (*see illustration*) each of which is quickly scanned by the eyes. The eyes ask the brain to 'trust us', and absorb what they see. Somehow, it is argued, the brain stitches the rectangles together and makes sense of the text therein.

Reading backwards is not too far removed from 'layered reading' and many people have acquired the ability to read backwards and forwards with equal facility. In the days of metal typesetting, veteran typesetters could read a text in any direction and even

PEOPLE began to laugh at movies at about the time motion pictures were invented. Although it wasn't difficult to laugh at what passed for drama in those early days, it was the short comedy subject that provided the main attraction for the thousands of kinetoscopes, motoscopes and other peepshow machines which in the 1890s projected the first flickering rays of the celluloid sunrise.

Then came *The Great Train Robbery* in 1903, a Western which ran and ran for eleven breathless minutes. Audiences were excited and spellbound and demanded more; and for a decade comedy took a back stalls seat to a flood of adventure and dramatic films which by 1914 had reached feature status – movies of four reels or more as against the 12-minute single-reeler.

Ironically, it was the very success of screen drama that brought about what is now nostalgically called the Golden Age of Silent Comedy. Although an estimated thousand million people went through the cinema turnstiles of the world during 1916, mostly to see melodramas, the novelty of the moving image was faltering. Competition in the industry was intense, and exhibitors searched desperately for something new to whet the appetites of their jaded patrons. The answer was found in the two-reel comedies which soon became more popular than the serious features they were designed to support. A new cinematic sub-industry was born.

Producers quickly formed companies specializing in comedy films and, drawing mainly from music halls and burlesque theatres, gathered around them anyone who could make people laugh. Mack Sennett was one of the first and most famous. Vitagraph was another, starting out with the genial, portly ex-Englishman John Bunny in 1910 and adding, in upside-down, so familiar were they with the shapes of the characters. This potential is put to work in a method which asks readers to read a line left to right, then the line below it right to left, then left to right and so on. This is exactly the way in which a word processor spits out its text, so the idea does not seem inappropriate to the computer age. It is also true that some languages require their users to read right to left or vertically: Chinese and Hebrew being just two examples.

The theoretical advantage in being able to read both ways is obvious: the elimination of the time taken for the eyes to travel back to the beginning of each line. That's 10–15,000 eye movements saved per average book: almost one mile of eye tracking. If you're convinced, you can start training by following your finger or hand along a line, down, back along the next line and so on. The moving finger is the key to mastering this particular skill.

Underlining

If you've seen people read with their finger or fingers on the page, you're witnessing an innocent version of a practice called 'underlining' which underpins quite a few speed-reading techniques.

In many ways, the use of the moving finger as a reading aid makes a certain amount of sense. It can help control stopping, regressing and wandering, and it can be used to pace your reading. It is easier to command your finger to move at a certain pace than your eyes, which often seem to have a will of their own. But while the use of the hand or finger can be most helpful to slow or disadvantaged readers by focusing their vision and concentration, if you are an average reader you would do well to leave your digits out of the reading process altogether unless you want to risk acquiring a bad habit.

Mechanical aids

The most ubiquitous device used to train people to read faster is the '*Tachistoscope*', an apparatus that flashes brief and accurately timed images to the viewer. When called a 'reading machine' the tachistoscope is fitted with slides of words and phrases which are flashed on a screen for a fraction of a second. The eyes are thus forced to recognise these words and phrases very quickly; whether or not the words and phrases are being read and understood is another matter. What seems to happen with this technique is that the concentration required for the exercises undoubtedly leads to increased reading speeds – for example, from 200 w.p.m. to 400 w.p.m. – but, alas, backsliding takes place and before long any increase in speed is lost. Tachistoscopes are usually made for laboratory or classroom use but hand-held models are also available (one marketed in the UK is called the 'Excel-O-Reader'), but their usefulness is open to question.

Other so-called reading machines include the 'Eye-span Trainer' which attempts to drill the eyes into grabbing wider and wider spans of words, and the 'Pace-Accelerator', a mechanical device that forces you to read at a predetermined accelerated speed.

The Pace-Accelerator is ingenious, if nothing else. The book or the text is placed under the machine and the user sets the desired w.p.m. speed. The machine is then switched on, a horizontal bar of light hits the top line of the text, and then proceeds to move down the page at the pre-set speed. If the pace is too fast the reader can slow it down, but the idea is that the eyes and brain will be stretched to the limit before the reader gives in. In theory the Pace-Accelerator appears to have its uses as a disciplinary device but in reality all it does is substitute for the human will in ordinary reading exercises. Some reading efficiency experts claim that such pacing machines lead to dependency and lowered comprehension.

More straightforward but ultimately more sophisticated training accessories are now available on film, videotape and computer software programmes. But, again, these merely replicate what can just as easily be taught on, and from, the printed page. Their main value is for classroom use, where a number of students can be taken through fixation exercises at one time, no doubt finding it a more stimulating experience than reading texts on a page. But in the final analysis, we do the bulk of our reading from the conventional printed page, so it makes sense to do our training on-site.

Soaring into 'super reading'

By far the most impressive course in the entire spectrum of speed reading is that developed many years ago by a Salt Lake City college counsellor named Evelyn Wood. Called the 'Evelyn Wood 7-Day Speed Reading & Learning Program', its unabashed claims include a guarantee that you'll increase your reading speed by at least 50% after just an hour's study and practice; that you'll double your speed in one week; that you'll remember everything you read; and that you'll be shown how to reach the speed reading 'stratosphere' of 1,200–3,000 w.p.m.

The reaction to such breathtaking claims is to dismiss them instantly. But the Evelyn Wood course can stake at least one claim without fear of contradiction: it has been around for over 30 years and continues to prosper. It therefore deserves serious examination.

The Evelyn Wood story begins in the 1950s, when her interest in reading speed was awakened by a college professor who, when given an 80-page paper to study overnight, handed it back in a matter of minutes; moreover, in a subsequent discussion, it was obvious he knew its content thoroughly. The professor then went on his way while Ms Wood, pondering on the phenomenon, estimated that he had consumed the text at the rate of about 2,500 w.p.m.

This intrigued her because it was then thought that the highest attainable reading speed was well under 1,000 w.p.m. Could this extraordinary ability be taught, she wondered?

Next, she launched a national quest for the country's fastest reader, and discovered some fifty people who could read at speeds ranging from 1,500 to 6,000 w.p.m. They were all interviewed at length but still the secrets of super reading eluded her.

Now for the pastoral interlude. One day in 1958 during a holiday, Evelyn Wood sat by a stream reading *Green Mansions*, doing her best to read it at speed. Becoming aware that it was well short of Olympian standards, she angrily flung the book down into the mud. Then, realising what a foolish action this was, she picked up the soiled book and attempted to read in a calmer state of mind. As she did so she began brushing the dried mud from the page with her hand.

Well, what do you think? At an ever-increasing pace her eyes, following the brushing hand, raced across the page. She turned the page and kept brushing, her eyes following the sweeping, brushing movements. The pages flipped by, faster and faster. Ten minutes and 50,000 words later she had finished what remained of *Green Mansions*. With a thumping heart, Evelyn made a calculation. She had been reading at the phenomenal rate of nearly 5,000 w.p.m. More importantly, she had discovered the secrets of super reading, a niche in speed reading folklore, and a small fortune.

The Evelyn Wood Reading Dynamics Institute was established in Washington in 1959 and since then, through its network of classes and publications, has inspired millions to try to reach those giddy heights.

The principles of the Evelyn Wood technique – called 'mental soaring' – are simply stated but difficult to nail down. Mental soaring, as defined by the Institute, is the 'high speed, super-efficient assimilation and organisation of printed materials'. To be an expert in mental soaring that will take you up into supersonic altitudes you have to leave some nasty habits behind. These include reading from left to right in the conventional manner, and what is termed the 'hidden voice': the propensity to silently voice the words you read.

In place of these old line-by-line, mental mumbling reading habits, you are trained in the 'visual-vertical' technique of reading. This completely excludes hearing the silent sounds as you read and concentrates exclusively on visual perception; also, like Evelyn Wood in 1958, you read with your eyes sweeping like broad brushstrokes vertically down the page.

The reason for this dramatic change in reading procedure is, according to the Institute, because 'subvocal linear' reading (silent voice, line by line) peaks at around 800 w.p.m. and it's no use trying to push any faster. After conversion to 'visual-vertical' reading, however, you can soar at supersonic speeds, first experiencing a 'rough patch' at between 900–1,200 w.p.m. as you shift back and forth between the two modes, and then accelerating to a consistent 1,500 w.p.m.

Other super readers, like the world champion Howard Berg, claim that reading at speeds of thousands of words a minute and a page a second is more an experience than a technique. The mind acquires a 'heightened state' to create a 'oneness of mind and text'. The text peels off the pages as a series of images rather than meaningful words and sentences. It requires, so say its devotees, a Zen philosophy of discipline, meditation and practice.

The use of 'mental soaring' and similar approaches to increase reading speed (they hardly address reading efficiency!) is not seriously considered beyond this chapter. This is not to imply disapproval, however, nor to suggest that such techniques don't work. They *have* worked for *some* people who, for reasons of their own, wish to read at prodigious speeds.

If your ambition is to become a verbal space cadet, the Evelyn Wood Institute is waiting for you. If, on the other hand, your wish is to speed up your reading, improve your comprehension and increase your reading enjoyment, then read on.

But we must begin with our feet on the ground. That's where any improvement in reading efficiency begins.

Final preparations

Before we finally embark on the programme to help increase reading speed and comprehension, let's do a last-minute check. If there's one thing we don't want on this voyage, it's a bad reading habit. And, without even knowing it, we can acquire quite a few.

Why do you want to read faster?

One bad habit in all of us is the propensity to go about certain activities without any defined sense of purpose. This is a sure recipe for inefficiency, dissatisfaction and boredom. So, at this point, ask yourself: *Why do I want to read faster?*

If you can't answer this satisfactorily, perhaps you should ask yourself why you are reading this book at all. Because, as in all enterprises that demand practice and dedication, you are going to need a target to aim at. Some objective that at present eludes you. Some ambition. Some *reason*!

Is the purpose to increase your capacity to absorb information to do with your job or career or a move up the promotion ladder? Is it because you are falling behind in your leisure reading; that you have piles of books stacked up and can't seem to ever get through them? Is it the desire to get through some study course in a year instead of two? Or is it simply because you have come to realise that you are a slow reader, and would like to do something about it? Whatever it is, try to define it, try to focus on it, and make that your *raison d'être* for the effort you are about to undertake.

Set yourself a target

When you have done this, the next step is to set yourself an attainable target in terms of reading speed and comprehension. From what you've read so far this shouldn't be too difficult. You have measured your reading speed and comprehension, and you are aware of what can be achieved. The question is: what do you think *you* can achieve? An extra 80 w.p.m. in reading speed? An extra 20% in your level of comprehension? Whatever it is, whatever you want to achieve and think you can succeed with some serious effort, write it down, *now*:

Reading speed (w.p.m.)	Comprehension (%)
Present ———— w.p.m.	———— %
Target ———— w.p.m.	———— %

Let this be your initial target, one that you feel comfortable with. Let it be your first stage. You can always set yourself a more ambitious target later on. Meanwhile, let's continue with the physical to check if you have any other bad habits.

Twitching, scratching and wriggling

To many people, the act of reading is an energetic physical experience. They squirm in their chair, wriggle constantly, scratch, massage parts of their body, twitch, slump, stretch and generally carry on as though such movements are as essential to the act of reading as seeing.

Such physical activity while reading is distracting and must also, over a long period, be very tiring. Many of these movements may also be tics, indicative of some problem or stress.

These unnecessary physical movements will ultimately stand in the way of improving reading efficiency simply by siphoning off the energy you need for fast reading and instant understanding of texts. Try to identify them and see what you can do to eliminate them. Comfortable chairs, good lighting and a private environment will all help, but most of all it will be your own willpower that will overcome these habits.

Mumbling and sub-vocalising

Sub-vocalising is a fancy speed-reading term for silent mumbling and muttering – moving the lips while reading.

If it could be measured, we probably mutter silently at about the same pace as we speak – around 150 w.p.m. So if as we read we also move our lips in sync with the words, we are forever anchoring our reading speed to 150 w.p.m.

How do you eliminate such a bad habit? There is no sure remedy. Holding a pencil in the teeth or chewing gum sometimes helps but, again, only willpower and conscious control over this surplus movement will ensure a permanent cure.

Loitering without intent

A very common habit among readers and especially slower readers, is wandering through a text, peeping ahead, glancing back, loitering for no good reason and often stopping for seconds at a time, the mind on some other planet.

Here's an illustration of the sight path of such an untidy reader. You will see instantly why such habits will severely inhibit even the slenderest effort to improve reading speed.

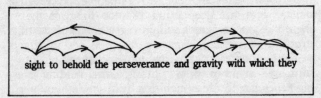

sight to behold the perseverance and gravity with which they

One of the most pernicious bad habits in reading is the 'peep', or the tendency for the eyes to dart forward to alight on a word, name or number that somehow attracts them. Look, for example, at this test text:

The fizz of the 'Jazz Age', which helped to invigorate America during the 1920s, was for most people in Britain a feeble, flat refreshment, its effervescence spent in the transatlantic crossing. The war had exhausted the country; capital was short and deprivation was everywhere. Industrial unrest broke out on a grand scale. Twenty-seven million working days were lost through strikes in 1920, and 2,000 strikes preceded the General Strike of 1926. Uneconomic industrial technology and antiquated manufacturing plant added to the problem. Over 70% of all Britain's coal was produced at a loss, and a Royal Commission decided the miner was the cause. While a mineowner like the Duke of Northumberland made over £80,000 a year profit when his miners worked and lived in the most deplorable conditions, the government nevertheless recommended a cut in miners' wages. It was this that precipitated the General Strike which, while it left a legacy of bitterness among millions of workers, hardly interrupted the lives of the privileged, who continued to yacht at Cowes, watch Eton play Harrow at Lords, present their debutante daughters to the King, and to visit Cannes, Biarritz and Le Touquet.

In a laboratory experiment with 15 people, no less than nine took a quick peep at the '£80,000' figure in the middle of the paragraph within two seconds of starting to read it. There are, most experts agree, certain trigger words like 'sex', or famous names, that speak out of turn, and it takes a lot of control to discipline the eyes, via the mind, to resist such time-wasting detours.

Regressing

Of all time-wasting habits, however, the one that clocks up most misspent time is undoubtedly 'skipping back', or regressing as it is called in the speed-reading trade. It has been estimated that many if not most people spend over 25% of their reading time in reverse. More scientifically, a 1970 study of the eye movements of thousands of students of all ages found that regressions ranged from 52 per 100 words with primary school pupils to 15 per 100 words with college students. The significance of this is that a reading speed of 300 w.p.m. with a 25% regression count could be a 400 w.p.m. speed if regression could be eliminated.

Nobody ever became a champion runner by running backwards a few metres several times during every lap, yet we tolerate this quite severe handicap in our reading. Obviously it is a habit that must be stamped out.

Opinion is divided as to how to eliminate regressing. Some instructors favour using the finger or hand to keep the eye on track. Others advocate running a piece of white card down the page, covering up the lines previously read. One reading school reports good results using a card with a narrow horizontal window cut out of it; the window just large enough to reveal half of one line.

Physical devices like these can certainly help by obscuring potential distractions and focusing concentration, but they cannot be used permanently. Sooner or later a reader with a bad regression habit has to tackle the problem with willpower and sheer determination.

Record your progress

With any form of instruction you do better if you have access to a record of your progress. This will tell you if you are, indeed, making progress or not, and at what rate.

The programme of instruction and exercises given in this book is essentially a self-study course, so you must keep your own record. You have already started by recording your present reading speed and comprehension rate.

It is essential that you record the results of your scores accurately as you move through the exercises and, later, the scores achieved by reading exercises you devise yourself.

A simple Progress Chart will be found on page 112, on which you can record all your scores.

Reading at speed: The basic techniques

You will have noticed that '*technique*' is used in the plural in the chapter heading. This is because there is, in enlightened reading-efficiency circles, a number of routines, all linked in purpose, some of which may work better for one individual than for others. But at the outset, you are urged to try them all.

For a start, we will return to fixations – those pauses during which the eyes see and recognise a word or words. The object is to recognise as many words as possible in a single fixation as fast as possible.

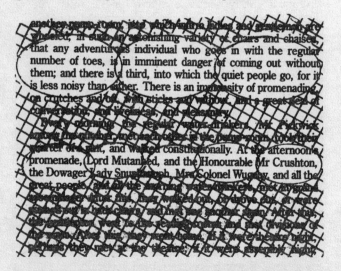

This diagram will refresh your memory about fixations. It shows the visual 'bites' made by a medium-to-fast reader, and also those made by a slow reader. The latter, you will see, records more fixations per line, larger overlaps, and regressions.

Our first exercise is to induce your eyes to make

broader fixations or larger bites. Try reading this paragraph by taking in each group of words with a single glance – and no looking back!

The peasants of   mid 19th century France   were the exhausted   survivors of a   2,000-year campaign of exploitation   and extermination   which began with   their enslavement   by the Romans   and continued through   centuries of serfdom,   injustice and misrule   by rapacious aristocrats.   Although the   Revolution of 1793   didn't pass the   peasants by,   its benefits did,   for when their serfdom   was exchanged   for land rights   they inherited   a harsher master   and mistress: money, and   the land itself.   They became   grist for the mills   of distant   city-based capitalism,   victims of supply and demand,   increasing taxes   and falling prices. But while money was   a ferocious taskmaster   the new mistress   was even crueller,   and more capricious. The land was   so impoverished that   no amount of work   could make it yield   one extra ear of grain.   A single hailstorm   could destroy   a year's hard labour.   Rain rotted the seed   and drought shrivelled   the growing corn.   Weeds poisoned   the soil and   cattle were   wiped out overnight   by any one of   a hundred disorders. Yet somehow the peasant survived.

If you didn't quite manage it first time around, have another try. When you succeed, you've made the first step in your quest for a faster reading pace.

Now try the same exercise in another format. In this, the groups of words are assembled vertically.

The arrival of
the railway train
in the 19th century
introduced a
new dimension to

terror and murder.
It is difficult
to convey today
the effect these
belching iron monsters
had on the population
over a century ago;
they steamed and roared
like angry serpents,
achieving speeds
unattainable by any
other form of transport,
shrieking through the night,
disappearing into
long, dark tunnels
and all too frequently
destroying themselves
and their passengers
in spectacular accidents.

Although you didn't time yourself, by taking in each
group of words at one bite you probably read this piece
at a speed much faster than you've ever achieved
previously!

But to hammer home this basic need to recognise
groups of words, the next exercise offers a helping
hand in the shape of a vertical line running down the
text. As you read your word groups, the line will help
you centre your visual span, adding further to fixation
efficiency.

Three thousand miles away
Alfred Dreyfus
endured an
unimaginable hell.
When he stepped ashore
on that blistering,
God forsaken
former leper colony

he had hope, but
little reason to believe
he would not be doomed
to die there.
As if the two-mile-long,
quarter-mile-wide island
wasn't prison enough,
a stone cell
had been built within
a wooden enclosure.
In this cruel cage he lived,
half-crazed by the heat,
tortured by insects,
numbed by the desolation.

Yes, the exercise demands some concentration, but it
surely demonstrates yet again the effectiveness of
reading groups of words.

If, however, you experienced some difficulty with
these three exercises, try these word stacks to see if we
can't seduce your eyes into accepting more extended
fixations. Read down vertically as fast as you can, but
make sure that you are actually seeing and recognising
every word.

Looking
back to
the early days
of the war,
with the Germans
only thirty miles
away, we seemed
oblivious to the
dangers that could lie
ahead. In the glorious
weather of the
summer of 1940 the work
proceeded as usual;
the binder cutting the corn

while, overhead, on those
August mornings, waves of bombers
with their fighter escorts regularly
passed on their way to
London with hardly any opposition.

This stacking technique of teasing the eyes to widen
their span has been in wide use for some time and has
proved successful in demonstrating that achieving
fixations with 50% wider visual spans is not only
possible, but probable.

To check on how these wider fixations affect your
reading speed, the next stacking exercise should be
timed. Make a note of the exact time on your watch
when you start, and again when you finish, because
those seconds will be important!

Reading Test No.4

START

When
Samuel March
died, and Henry's
sole succession to
the garden became fact,
with all the legal paper
trimmings and trappings
as unarguable evidence,
the family storm broke over
poor Henry's head in bitter
torrents of pleas, insults and
acrimony. All of them, they
said, had poured their sweat
into the making of
the now profitable orchard;
all of them, they said,
had worked their fingers
to the bone for years

in the belief that
they would be fairly treated
to an equal share
when the old man died –
and the fact that several
of them had married
and had moved to live elsewhere
in no way diluted
the righteousness of their claims.
Two of the daughters,
sensing the hopelessness and
bitterness that lay ahead,
grabbed what they could
in the way of removables,
clothes, jewellery and so forth, and
departed from the unhappy scene for good.
But the others hovered around
like angry dragonflies,
buzzing threateningly but helpless in the
face of the edict
of their father's last will and testament.

STOP!

Now note the time taken and check it against the Speed
Table on page 109. It is difficult to imagine that anyone
would have taken more than 40 seconds to read the
piece and, if so, then a course of remedial reading
should be undertaken before proceeding further. More
likely, you will have taken 30 seconds or less – in which
case your reading speed will be 340 w.p.m. or better.
You will note from the Speed Table, incidentally, that
as you clip the seconds off, your speed goes up at a
faster and faster rate; if your time was 20 seconds then
you read the piece at exactly 516 w.p.m.!

Although this form of exercise tends to enhance
w.p.m. speeds it is still worth recording on the
Progress Chart on page 112 to remind you later what
you can achieve.

By now you are, on occasions, taking bite-size fixations about the width of a newspaper column. The width of these differ (the tabloids being narrower) but average around 30 characters a line. Time the next exercise accurately and while your first concern is to read fast you should take care to understand what you are reading. To help you keep your eyes centred the columns each have a line running down the middle. Second hand noted, deep breath, and lots of concentration!

THERE is no more unattractive a trait to witness than self-satisfaction. Yet, one of the more attractive sensations is a sweet smugness. Such a sensation I experienced only a few days ago, as I glided through rush-hour traffic to an early meeting, streaming past queues of jammed cars, lorries and buses.

The morning was one of those perfect autumnal examples – blue skies and clear, sharp air – as I headed over Chelsea Bridge, smiling graciously at the unfortunates on the buses' lower decks, nodding to fuming drivers. A serenity I have rarely known imbued my spirit as I left the traffic lights ahead of the queue. I was travelling on the back of a bike – a taxi bike.

It is the brainchild of Robert Cave, a former Warburg stockbroker, who ferried many of his clients about during the Tube strikes of 1988. But he didn't seriously start investigating the potential of a bike for hire until the beginning of last year. By November his scheme had won the Business Innovation award sponsored by The Sunday Times and Honeywell. Now two taxi bikes ply their trade on the streets of the capital.

I booked Robert Cave and his two-wheel transport alternative last week, to test its speed and efficiency and to find out what the damned helmet would do to the hair. If only I had the money I would buy the charming Mr Cave and his bike for life – I haven't had such fun with more clothes on than usual since . . . and I wasn't late for one appointment.

The first advantage is that you don't have to look like a down-market Terminator. You can wear your ordinary clothes (although a tiny Lycra skirt may be chilly), as Robert provides a choice of jacket (heavy or light), gloves and the adjustable helmet complete with its own microphone so you can chat away to your driver or just quietly shriek into it as you watch one of those nice Parcel Force vans heading straight for you. The fear evaporates as you gain confidence, and realise it's not going to further your driver's career should as little as one toenail of yours be chipped.

A waterproof, windproof rug affair (rather like the

tartan jobs you see covering the Queen's knees in her open carriages) covers your legs and is snapped into place. Briefcase, handbags et al are stored under your seat which comes complete with backrest. Once you are helmeted, wired up and snapped in, the fun starts.

The usual crawl of traffic north over Chelsea Bridge was as nothing as we headed straight for the top of the queue, and were off the minute the traffic lights changed. A journey that can normally take at least 30 minutes was accomplished in 14.

Again, check your time and read off your w.p.m. rate from the Speed Table on page 110. Don't be surprised if, this time, your speed is lower than that achieved with Exercise No. 4. Newspaper columns provide excellent practice material but they also contain many broken or hyphenated words which have to be mentally joined up again.

Nevertheless, your speed should be well up on your initial reading speed, perhaps even by 100 w.p.m.

The next exercise takes us a little further down the newspaper column road because this time there will be no centre line. Some people find the centre line a help, others a hindrance, which is why, from the variety of techniques, you are encouraged to select and work with those that help you the most.

The next exercise also includes a comprehension test, so don't sacrifice understanding for the sake of sheer speed! Don't forget to make a note of your start and finish times.

Reading Exercise No.6

Tuscany is where the best olive oil is said to come from – if you're talking to someone from Tuscany that is – and to travel round the region during November and December, when the olives ripen, is to see the picking and pressing process in full swing.

'St Martin's day is when the season starts,' shouted one picker from high in a tree near Castello di Montecchio (although exactly when St Martin's day was he wasn't sure). He poked his head out of the branches and shrugged: 'All you need to know is that the best olives in Tuscany come from this hillside.' Then, like everyone involved with olive oil, he launched into an account of the great freeze of 1985.

That year, a severe cold spell hit Tuscany and a large proportion of the trees died. The landscape was devastated. Production almost came to a halt. Subsequently, a scandal emerged when it was discoverted that manufacturers had imported oil from other regions, bottled it, and sold it at Tuscan prices. Further cold spells in following years did more damage and the industry is still nowhere near recovery. Last year's crop was 80% down on the pre-1985 average.

Not that this has had any effect on the 'olive fever' that surfaces annually in these parts, as local folk take time off and spend it up a tree, keen to be involved in the picking process. The collection of the olive crop is a rural tradition, and well–respected – by the older generation anyway – as the last vestige of *mezzadria*,

the age-old share-cropping system whereby landowners would employ pickers to bring in the harvest, and then pay them with half of what they collected.

In all other departments of farming in Italy, technology has meant the redundancy of this system, and of most of the *contadini* (the peasant farmers). But, come the olive-picking season, those who still have an interest return to the land. And with good reason. So labour intensive is the work, and so expensive the end product, that spending a few weeks up a tree can turn out rather lucrative.

I came across groups of these pickers on a day of hill-walking above the town of Cortona. Tuscany can get cold at this time of year and, in the valley, the cold brings fog. But I was walking above it all, and the pickers were working under a crisp, blue sky.

In one grove an entire family were up ladders with nets spread out beneath the trees, raking the branches so that the fruit fell gently, with the sound of raindrops. 'The best olives in Italy come from this hillside,' said one man, and he explained how in Tuscany the olives are superior because they are picked off the trees by hand, unlike other regions such as Calabria, where farmers beat the trees with sticks to bring the fruit down – thus bruising it. Olives need to be hand picked to assure the correct ripeness. Pick too soon and you get a low yield of oil; too late and the oil is greasy and bitter.

That's the theory. In practice, the pickers seem to grab at whatever they can, whenever they can, the weather being the determining factor. 'You can't pick in the fog,' explained a voice from the branches. 'Nor in the rain,' and he did his best to mime the word 'mildew'.

When you've noted your reading time, check it against the Speed Table on page 110 for your w.p.m. speed. Now, without looking again at the exercise test, answer the following questions.

Comprehension Test No. 6

1. When do olives ripen? **a**. April–May; **b**. August–September; **c**. November–December
2. When was the 'great freeze' which damaged many olive trees? **a**. 1989; **b**. 1985; **c**. 1981
3. Where is the best olive oil supposed to come from? **a**. Tuscany; **b**. Umbria; **c**. Florence
4. The olive trees are located: **a**. in the valleys; **b**. on the hillsides; **c**. in the ravines
5. In Calabria, the olives are harvested: **a**. by picking; **b**. by pulling; **c**. by beating with sticks
6. Olives picked too soon: **a**. rot; **b**. give inferior oil; **c**. give a low oil yield
7. Olives picked in the rain develop: **a**. mildew; **b**. a greasy feel; **c**. mezzadria
8. When does the olive season start? **a**. St Martin's Day; **b**. Saint's Day; **c**. just after Easter
9. Last year's crop was well down on the average. Was it: **a**. 50% down; **b**. 60% down; **c**. 80% down?

10. The olives are picked by: **a**. Turkish migrant
    workers; **b**. local people; **c**. imported labour from
    Rome

Check the answers on page 108 and award 10
percentage points for each correct answer. The total,
out of 100%, will give you your comprehension score
for Exercise 6. Record it, with your w.p.m. speed, on
the Progress Chart on page 112.

At this point in the programme you should spend a
few days practising with newspaper columns, ideally
short general articles. Time each reading and work out
your speed using the following formula:

$$\frac{\text{Number of words}}{\text{Time in seconds}} \times 60 = \text{w.p.m.}$$

When you are hitting a consistent speed which
represents the sort of improvement that pleases or
satisfies you, then it is time to move on.

Not all your reading will consist of the columns of
newspapers. Much of it will be in the form of books,
journals, magazines, memos and so on. With these the
average line is likely to contain from 50 to 80
characters, so you must adapt your fixations to take this
into account. But if you can handle a newspaper
column with a full line fixation, you should be able to
read a line from a paperback page (averaging 50–60
characters per line) with just two fixations. This will be
our next step.

For our next exercise we are looking at a narrow-
format paperback page with a width of less than 45
characters. But to encourage you to read each line with
two fixations only, it is divided into two parts. Each
line is also separated from the others by a larger than
usual space, which should help you keep your eyes on
track without wandering above and below the line.

There may or may not be a comprehension test on this text, so, while reading as fast as you can, try also to take in the important points of what is being said.

Reading Exercise No.7

Make a note of your start and finish times.

If Disneyland can be seen
of the psychological
wonderland, booby trapped
and other obsessive themes,
do psychologists think
with television now the
entertainment of children,
and benefits of comics –
papers and newspapers –
But the comic child of
society today. Most
now middle-aged, many of
and influence in the
other they in turn were
weekly comic paper –
Wonder, Chips, Radio Fun,
others – not only in
but also in their manner
communicating. How many of
which may be traced back
innocent comic strip they
many find it difficult to
experience has shown them
have trouble coming to
arguable tenets of feminism

through an extreme edge
prism as a sort of Freudian
with oral, castration
then what on earth
about comics? Fortunately
dominant medium for the
the debate on the dangers
in comic books, comic
is now much less relevant.
yesterday is the pillar of
former readers of comics are
them in positions of power
community. To some degree or
influenced by their favourite
it might have been *Funny
Knockout* or any one of 100
their attitudes to society
of thinking and
them have made decisions,
to attitudes nurtured by an
hardly remember? How
suppress prejudices their
are wrong? How many
terms with even the least
and equality?

Record the time taken to read this, check it against the Speed Table on page 110 for your w.p.m., and record the result on your Progress Chart. Don't be too disappointed if your speed has dropped; in fact it would be astonising if it hadn't, because by asking you to read each line with just two visual bites the exercise has demanded a strenuous effort on your part.

At about 45 characters the lines in that exercise were comparatively narrow. It is more likely that you'll meet the 50-plus characters-per-line format typical of paperbacks, and this is the format we'll deal with next.

But before we do there is a subsidiary exercise that may help you with your 'two bites a line' practice.

Don't marginalise

Eye tracking research has helped us identify wasted visual effort in the reading process. We know this occurs with regressions, wandering, peeping ahead and so on. We know that time is needed simply to return the eye from the end of one line to the beginning of the next. Some of this unproductive time can be converted but some – like the eye-return movement, unless you are prepared to learn to read backwards – cannot.

But there is one area of wasted eye movement that we *can* attend to and that is the time our eyes spend in the margins of texts. One estimate suggests that an average reader can spend 20–30% of his reading time in the blank margins!

The reason for this is simple. When our eyes return to the beginning of each line the tendency is to focus on the first word; this becomes the centre of our first fixation for that line. If it is the centre of what would normally be a three- or four-word fixation, it is clear that the left half will be preoccupied with nothing but blank space. Such a fixation is taking in only one or two words instead of three or four. And the same principle applies to the other end of the line.

It's important to be conscious of the potential for margins to waste reading time. But if this habit is natural and probably ingrained, what can we do about it?

that he felt a great deal better) whereat his friends were very

What can be done is to move the centre of your fixations
a word or half a dozen characters in from each end of
the line. You may be able to do this mentally, or you
may at first need the help of a couple of indented lines
drawn down the page.

Try reading the next text by moving the focus of
your fixations inside the vertical rules, still reading each
line with just two fixations.

and piercing; his cheek-bones were high and prominent; and
his jaws were so long and lank, that an observer would have
supposed that he was drawing the flesh of his face in, for a
moment, by some contraction of the muscles, if his half-opened
mouth and immovable expression had not announced that it was
his ordinary appearance. Round his neck he wore a green shawl,
with the large ends straggling over his chest, and making their
appearance occasionally beneath the worn button-holes of his
old waistcoat. His upper garment was a long black surtout; and
below it he wore wide drab trousers, and large boots, running
rapidly to seed.

We are now going to tackle a fairly standard 60
characters-per-line text. This exercise will take you
quite a way forward and will place considerable
demands on your concentration. As with Exercise No.7
each line is divided into two parts, and each part will
constitute a single fixation. Don't be in too much of a
hurry; while keeping in mind all you've learned about
speed, remember that you read to absorb information.
You should accurately record your reading time, and
although your w.p.m. rate will almost certainly be
slower than with some of the previous exercises, don't
be despondent. What you're doing now is mastering a
technique. Once you've mastered it, practice will soon
bring you up to speed.

The country houses of the English aristocracy provided first the birthplace and subsequently the nursery for the emerging pastime of photography. The inhabitants of these houses were, after all, among the fortunate few with the time, the money, and the facilities for the demanding techniques of early photographic art. So it is in the trove of albums and scrapbooks recently unearthed in the libraries and attics of stately homes that we find the forerunners of today's snapshots – photographs taken for amusement rather than profit and with an exploratory enthusiasm rather than an urge to create 'art'.

And while the quickly established commercial branch of photography petrified hundreds of thousands of faces and groups posed before stylised studio backdrops, it was the amateur, in those early years, who recorded the environment, fashions, interests, and especially the family life of the mid-Victorian period. Then, at the turn of the century, followed the more humble owners of those millions of cheap cameras, without pretensions and aspirations other than the desire to snap a picture and the hope for a viewable result. With hindsight, we now realise that the truest of all photographic images taken over the past century have come from this often ridiculed group.

Make a note of your reading time, consult the Speed Table for the w.p.m. rate, and enter the result on your Progress Chart. But to repeat: don't be disappointed if it has dropped considerably; you'll soon pick it up with practice.

Practice, practice, practice

You've now earned a breather. Well, not exactly a breather, but a respite from further instruction. You've come a long way. You've acquired some knowledge of speed reading, reading speeds, comprehension levels, the roles of the eyes, mind and memory, visual span and fixations and a variety of techniques to improve your reading efficiency. You may have been exhilarated by the way your reading speed has increased through the exercises; or perhaps a shade disappointed.

But what you most certainly do have now is a valuable portfolio of basic techniques for reading faster and understanding more. It's up to you – and you alone – to benefit from them. And that means practice, practice, practice.

You can put this book aside for a week or so if you wish while you put its principles to work. Several short sessions a day are usually best. Last thing at night, when you're tired and your energy and concentration levels are low, is best used for sleeping. Test yourself with texts chosen from a variety of sources: newspapers, magazines, trade journals, textbooks, even novels. Set yourself slabs of between 1,000–2,000 words, or roughly three to eight pages of a book. Count the words in ten lines, divide by ten and you have the average number of words per line. Count the lines per page, multiply by the average, and you have the number of words per page. Thus

10 lines	96 words
Average	9.6 words
32 lines per page	
9.6 × 32 =	307 words
6 pages =	1,842 words

For your word per minute rate, use the formula on page 67.

Further tips

Throughout the remainder of *The Secrets of Speed Reading* we will discuss a number of ways that will help you in your efforts to read even faster and to raise your comprehension levels.

Meanwhile, here are a few tips you might like to think about.

Verbal Fixations   Many highly literate people may find it difficult to divide a line of words in an arbitrary fashion. Long conditioning to reading grammatical phrases may act as an inhibiting factor in the 'two fixations a line' technique. Such people may find that tailoring their fixations to grammatical phrases may work best for them. For example, two lines divided into purely visual fixations might subdivide like this:

As with our surnames, Britain's / stock of first names grew in size and variety with / successive invasions;

For many people there will be a tendency to resist such a brutal division; for them a more logical division might be:

As with our surnames, / Britain's stock of first names grew in size and variety / with successive invasions;

If grammatically-based fixations suit you and you are making good progress, you would be well advised to continue as you are. In fact, recognising which words are important and unimportant in phrases is a further development of basic speed-reading technique which will be discussed later in this book.

The 'Quick Return'   Although earlier we poured cold water on the notion that the eyes can be trained to move rhythmically, you can exercise some degree of control over your eye movements while reading. In particular, many reading efficiency students find that they can discipline their eyes to move quickly and smoothly from the end of a line to the beginning of the next. As this is a movement made thousands of times in an hour or two of reading, it is worth some conscious effort to keep it short and to resist wandering elsewhere on the page.

Loss of Comprehension   Almost inevitably, the sheer effort required to significantly increase your reading speed will rob you of the energy and concentration required to understand to the full what you are reading. A lowering of comprehension is typical at this stage – but the next chapter will demonstrate that any loss need only be temporary.

Improving comprehension

It was popularly said of former American President Gerald Ford that he couldn't walk and chew gum at the same time.

Right now many of us could be in a similar position: while we've gained in reading speed our comprehension has dropped a few percentage points. Not everyone can perform two disparate acts equally well at the same time.

However, the instruction and exercises should have us poised for a three-way improvement – in concentration, reading speed, and comprehension. From this point, it is important that our performance in all three advances together.

It is equally important to understand that comprehension – the capacity to grasp an idea and retain it – is a conscious act. Of course, for some of us it is easier than for others, but we can all work at it to the best of our ability.

What's the big idea?

Although not strictly true, every sentence contains a thought and every paragraph projects an idea. A skilled reader will very quickly sort the wheat from the chaff, discarding the latter and retaining the essentials – the ideas and facts.

For example, see if you can identify the central idea of this paragraph:

The reason why many people object to ending sentences with prepositions can be traced back to the influence of Latin grammar on English; in Latin, ending a sentence with a preposition was frowned upon. Generations of scholars upheld the rule, although when masters of the language like Shakespeare (*Hamlet*: 'No traveller returns, puzzles the will/And makes us rather bear those ills we have/ Then fly to others that we know not of?') started hanging them out to dry, the big rethink on prepositions began. The modern view is that unless they send jarring notes to the ear, let them stay. A sentence like 'That's the restaurant we ate in' is perfectly respectable. Quite often, extremely clumsy locutions result from straining to avoid finishing with a preposition – demonstrated neatly by Winston Churchill when, criticising some civil servant's prose, he commented: 'This is the sort of English up with which I will not put.'

So, in a short phrase, what's the big idea in this long paragraph? It is, simply, *that it is now thought acceptable to end a sentence with a preposition provided it doesn't jar.*

Now, while some readers may struggle with such a paragraph, others will get the point in a flash. Why is this?

There's no specific answer, but efficient readers certainly have the knack of instantly isolating essentials in a text, while still reading the non-essential matter for flavour and interest. Here is how such a reader might focus in on what looks to be essential in the above paragraph:

The reason why many people **object to ending sentences with prepositions** can be traced back to the influence of Latin grammar on English; in **Latin**, ending a sentence with a preposition was **frowned upon**. Generations of scholars upheld the rule, although when masters of the language like **Shakespeare** (*Hamlet*: 'No traveller returns, puzzles the will/And makes us rather bear those ills we have/ Then fly to others that we know not of?') started hanging them out to dry, the big **rethink** on prepositions began. The **modern view** is that **unless they send jarring notes to the ear, let them stay.** A sentence like 'That's the restaurant we ate in' is perfectly respectable. Quite often, extremely **clumsy locutions result from straining to avoid finishing with a preposition** – demonstrated neatly by Winston Churchill when, criticising some civil servant's prose, he commented: 'This is the sort of English up with which I will not put.'

If by the end of that paragraph a reader has understood and retained the matter in bold type, that reader can move on with the knowledge that he or she has absorbed the main point of what the writer was saying. The other matter in the paragraph is interesting and supports and illustrates the writer's argument, but it is not essential. If you can train yourself to be observant in identifying essentials, and ruthless in discarding irrelevancies, both your speed and your comprehension will benefit considerably.

Understanding is the key

When reading fast there is, with beginners anyway, an understandable temptation to gloss over difficult bits – especially abstract concepts. Such readers arrive at the end of a paragraph or text and then the realization dawns that something's awry: they haven't understood it!

If you're driving a car and you come to a difficult bit, like a hill, you drop down a gear and slow down. The same applies to reading. You simply can't read, understand and retain a complex idea with the speed that you might breeze through a long stretch of undemanding text. Sometimes facts come in the form of names, numbers, dates, times, sizes and quantities, which can be extremely relevant – if they are, there must be a momentary pause to assimilate them.

The result of undigested reading is often the need to regress, or worse, the necessity for re-reading an entire slab of text until the light of understanding suddenly glows. It is all a waste of time and, as far as reading efficiency is concerned, quite counter-productive.

Be alert, be interested

There is no magic formula for improving the ability to understand, retain and recall, only some commonsense advice. If you can will yourself to be interested in what you are reading, you will be surprised how wonderfully everything falls into place. Being interested means following the writer closely, even critically, and thinking all the time about what is being presented to you in the form of words.

After all, if you're not interested in what you're reading, why are you reading it at all? There seems no point in such an exercise. Even if it's a long, tortuous memo; a heavy technical paper you have to study; or a set of instructions on how to assemble a cupboard – if you've set yourself the task of reading, you should do so with an alert and receptive mind. Such a state of mind will also protect you from wasting time reading worthless texts by signalling the pointlessness of continuing.

Anticipation

If you discipline yourself to be interested in what you read you will very likely acquire an aptitude to anticipate.

This is a real bonus for efficient readers, and is the facility to comprehend the emergence of an idea and then to leap over intervening and unessential matter to the conclusion and complete comprehension.

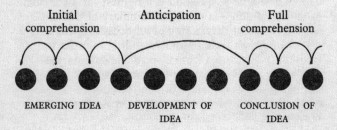

Initial	Anticipation	Full
comprehension		comprehension

EMERGING IDEA   DEVELOPMENT OF   CONCLUSION OF
              IDEA   IDEA

Anticipation is, to some degree or other, ever present in the reading process. When we read the title of a text we can anticipate what it is about. The name of the author may also lead us to anticipate what is in store for us. It's a native ability that's worth developing, so that during our reading we are constantly picking up clues to help us predict what is ahead. And because anticipating is also *thinking*, it keeps us deeply involved and receptive. Being aware of this, and consciously building it into your reading routine, will take you another big step ahead in your ability to read efficiently.

Comprehension tests

Tests to determine comprehension are, it has to be said, a most inexact science. Still, they do serve to demonstrate, quite disconcertingly at times, that there is more to speed reading than mere speed. They are also useful in giving the student some idea of his or her progress.

So far we have used three of four types of comprehension test:

- The YES/NO question – the most simplistic of all
- The multiple choice question (a, b or c) – a very basic form of question in which recognition of a correct answer does not necessarily indicate full comprehension
- The individual answer question – this asks for an exposition in the respondent's own words, and is a truer guide to level of comprehension

The fourth type of question is a request for a statement of understanding – a précis or summary of the text. This is the most demanding of all because it requires a sufficiently high level of understanding in order to translate a text into a factual, readable summary.

All four styles of test are used in this book, but, ultimately, any evaluation of your level of comprehension will rest with your own judgment and honesty.

Evaluation and practice

It is now time to put theory to the test, but before you embark on more exercises you ought to have some idea of your level of reading ability.

Although the following figures are based on the averaged results of a wide range of speed-reading students, and thus represent the basis for a fair comparison, they should still be treated with caution. Some people attempting a reading efficiency course make immediate progress but plateau quite quickly; others are slow starters and almost give up until – *click!* – they take off. Even in the speed-reading world there are hares and tortoises.

Check your progress on this chart:

If your speed at commencement was	After 1 week it should be	After 2 weeks it should be
Under 250 w.p.m.	275 w.p.m.	300 w.p.m.
250–300 w.p.m.	350 w.p.m.	375 w.p.m.
350–400 w.p.m.	400 w.p.m.	480 w.p.m.
Above 400 w.p.m.	+ 20%	+ 25%

The above assumes that you have absorbed the instruction and have not only diligently practised the exercises in this book but also undertaken a reasonable amount of extra reading at speed. It also assumes an average comprehension level in the 50–70% band.

If your own results measure up to the expectations shown in the chart, you can proceed with some satisfaction. With a little more guidance and a lot more practice, you can easily double your present attainment and possibly triple it or better.

If, however, your results aren't quite up to the mark,

run through this checklist to see if you can identify the problem that's holding up progress:

No change or very little improvement in speed?	☐
Comprehension level the same?	☐
Comprehension level lower?	☐
Problem concentrating? Eyes and mind wandering?	☐
Are you still regressing; unable to control regressions?	☐
Are you still reading word by word?	☐
Are your fixations still limited to 1/2/3 words at a time?	☐

Perhaps you've tried your best or perhaps you haven't tried hard enough, but all the problems above are curable and all the answers will be found in the previous pages. Search them out, go over them again, but, above all, grit your teeth, concentrate, and PRACTISE!

The following two exercises are to be read at your fastest possible speed, but remember that the emphasis will be on comprehension.

Reading Exercise No. 9

This is a review of *The Secret History*, a novel by Donna Tartt, by Penny Perrick, Fiction Editor of *The Sunday Times*. Make a note of the exact time on your watch and START!

An amoral gaiety rustles through this striking first novel, written with a brilliant casualness of tone, bright and flat and episodic rather than epic, in spite of the book's challenging length.

It's a murder story of sorts – a student of a posh but undisciplined college in upstate Vermont gets pushed over a ravine by his five best friends to stop him revealing an earlier murder – but the death doesn't shock or disturb; it's a bit of bad behaviour that the grown-ups mustn't be allowed to find out about, the sort of thing that Enid Blyton's Famous Five or Richmal Crompton's William and the Outlaws might have got up to if they had been brought up by parents who were nutty or violent or missing, the way that Tartt's killer kids were. These deadly little demons plan what they will later refer to as 'that other business' with an appealing curiosity and gusto that gives the story the hilarious gravity of comic-book capers.

Even young writers sometimes create 20-year-olds who have all the completed settledness of middle-age, but Tartt, who is 29, gives her characters a raw and jerky authenticity; she has the exact feel of anxious, pretentious youth, the swings between callous sophistication and childish panic. She knows how 20-year-olds can sleep the clock round beneath musty sheets, their strange diet: 'left-over *hors d'oeuvres* and a piece of birthday cake', 'cream cheese and marmalade sandwiches', 'maraschino cherries from a jar', their cheesy lack of housekeeping: 'Cigarette butts floated in a gin glass. There was a black, bubbled scorch in the varnish of the night table.'

The narrator is Richard Papen, dismally raised in a Californian hick town unlike the rest of the group he falls in with at Hampden College, who are rich and lofty and look like Calvin Klein advertisements. These are the chosen scholars who take the course in Greek offered by a campy tutor, Julian Morrow, who dangerously encourages their sense of specialness. Papen gains admittance to the *crème de la crème* because his Greek is good and he's willing to act the role of awed and obliging gopher; hardly a page goes by without Henry, Bunny (before he becomes a corpse), Francis, Charles or Camilla bursting into his room, waking him from one of his mega-naps and saying, 'I'm sorry to disturb you, but this is very important. I have a favour to ask of you.' Or, 'Listen. I want to ask you something. Will you do me a favour?' They take everything from him: a can of Coke he's just bought, a chemical formula for poison when Henry, the group's leader, is toying with the idea of feeding Bunny with deadly mushrooms – and, finally, his innocence.

Hampden College is a microcosm of a disordered and meaningless universe, where wearing the wrong kind of tie is as high on the list of *faux pas* as being hauled in for murder, which, as Henry, the most malign and stylish of the killers, explains, can always be thought of 'as redistribution of matter'.

Tartt provides glinting little thumbnail sketches of the kind of creative parenting that produced these weirdos. 'My mother was on some kind of yoga kick and she yanked me out of my old school in Boston and packed me off to this terrible place in Switzerland . . . Everyone wore sandals with socks. There were classes in dervish dancing and the cabbala.' The ghastliness of Bunny's family is more fully explored at his funeral, when his mother declares, 'if I've learned one thing from this it is never to order flowers from Sunset Florists again', and his father perks up at the graveside when a highly rated acquaintance shows up.

The Secret History is a very flashy novel; Tartt's erudition sprinkles the text like sequins, but she's such an adept writer that she's able to make the occasional swerve into Greek legends and semantics seem absolutely crucial to the examination of contemporary society which this book undoubtedly and seriously is, for all the fun it provides on the way.

Record your reading time, check it against the Speed Table on page 111 for your w.p.m., and enter the result on your Progress Chart. Now, without referring to the text, answer the following questions:

Comprehension Test No. 9

1. Who was the author of the novel?   _____

2. Name two of the characters mentioned   _____

3. Name one of the yucky foods they ate   _____

4. Who was the narrator?   _____

5. Much of the action is set in Hampden College. In which US state is it?   _____

6. Who is the leader of the pack?   _____
7. What's the title of the novel?   _____
8. Which of these names isn't mentioned in the review? Calvin Klein, Pizza Hut, Enid Blyton?   _____
9. Does the reviewer like the book?   _____
10. Who gets killed?   _____

Check the answers on page 108 and award yourself 10 percentage points for each one you get correct. The total will be your comprehension score for this exercise; enter it on your Progress Chart.

Now, have a short breather and compose yourself for the next exercise.

Reading Exercise No.10

This is a translation by David Hughes and Marie-Jacqueline Mason of a notorious passage from Emile Zola's 1873 novel *Le Ventre de Paris* ('The Belly of Paris'). In it, Zola describes a butter and cheese stall in Les Halles, the famous former Parisian produce market. Note the time on your watch, take a deep breath (not too deep, as you will see) and – START!

All around her the cheeses were stinking. On the two shelves at the back of the shop enormous blocks of butter were lined up; butter from Brittany was overflowing its baskets; Norman butters, wrapped in canvas, looked like sketches of bellies on to which a sculptor had thrown wet rags; other mounds, already in use, cut by large knives into sharp-pointed rocks full of valleys and crevices, had the appearance of summits in collapse, gilded with the pale light of an autumn evening. Under the display counter of red marble veined with grey, baskets of eggs suggested the whiteness of chalk, and in their crates on wicker trays, bung-shaped cheeses from Neufchâtel were placed end to end, and *gournays*, laid flat like medallions, brought expanses of more sombre colour, stained with their greenish tints. But for the most part the cheeses stood in piles on the table. There, next to the one-pound packs of butter, a gigantic *cantal* was spread on leaves of white beet, as though split by the blows of a hatchet; then followed a Cheshire cheese the colour of gold, a *gruyère* like a wheel fallen from some barbaric chariot, some Dutch cheeses as round as heads from the block smeared in dried blood, with that hardness of an empty skull which has earned them the nickname of 'dead-head'. A *parmesan* added its aromatic sting to the thick, dull smell of cooked pastry. Three *bries*, on round boards, had the melancholy look of extinguished moons: two, extremely dry, were at the full; the third was in its second quarter, running, creeping out in a white cream which spread into a lake, making havoc of the thin boards which had been put there in a vain attempt to hold it in check. Some *port-saluts*, shaped like the ancient discus, showed the names of their makers inscribed round the perimeter. A *romantour*, dressed in its silver paper, made one think of a bar of nougat, a squared cheese which had strayed into this realm of bitter fermentations. The *roqueforts*, too, under their crystal bells, were of princely aspect with their fat, marbled faces veined in blue and yellow, as though the victims of some shameful disease common to rich people who have eaten too many truffles; while on a dish, at one side of them, stood the goat's-milk cheese, as big as a child's fist, hard and grey like the pebbles which the rams start rolling at the angles of stony paths as they lead their flock. And then there were the smells: the pale yellow *mont d'ors* exhaled a sweetish odour; the *troyes*, very thick and bruised at the edges, of a harshness already stronger than the others, adding the fetid stench of a damp cellar; the *camemberts* with their scent of game too far gone; the *neufchâtels*, the *limbourgs*, the *marolles*, the *pont-l'évèques*, each one playing its own shrill note in a phrase that was harsh to the point of nausea; the *livarots*, dyed red, as terrible to the throat as the fumes of sulphur; and then, above all the others, were the *olivets*, wrapped in walnut leaves in the fashion of those decaying carcasses which peasants cover with branches on the edge of a field, steaming in the sun. The warm afternoon had turned the cheeses soft; the mould on the rinds was melting and glazing over with the rich colours of red copper and verdigris, like wounds that have badly healed; under the oak leaves, a breeze lifted the skin of the *olivets*, which heaved like a breast, with a slow deep breathing of a man asleep; a flood of life had driven a hole in a *livarot*, which gave birth through this gash to a people of worms. And behind the scales a *géromé* sewn with aniseed in its narrow box spread such an infection around it that flies had fallen dead by the box on the red marble veined with grey.

Immediately note your reading time, check it against the Speed Table on page 111 for your w.p.m., and enter it on your Progress Chart. Now, without referring in any way to the text, answer the following questions.

Comprehension Test No. 10

1. Was there any mention of an English cheese? _____

2. The size of some goats' milk cheeses was likened to what? _____

3. Some cheeses suggested decapitated heads. Where did they come from? _____

4. What was an Italian cheese mentioned? _____

5. Was it morning or afternoon? _____

6. Which cheese was melting into a creamy lake flowing over its wooden barriers? _____

7. Was butter mentioned in the passage? _____

8. The stinking *olivets* were compared to what? _____

9. The evil-smelling, aniseed-flavoured *géromé* had an unusual effect. What was it? _____

10. The display counter was made of what? _____

This is as much an exercise in memory and recall as comprehension, and it may have taken you by surprise. But nevertheless check the answers on page 108, award the usual 10 percentage points for each one you get correct, and enter the result on your Progress Chart.

And if your recall wasn't what it should have been, pay extra attention to the next chapter.

Improving – what was it? – recall

Is your memory like a sieve? Is your recall button on the blink? Before you rush to a conclusion, let's try to find out.

We'll do this with a little test, very much like the old party game. It consists of a list of 40 words, and you are allowed just 15 seconds to read them – a speed, incidentally, that's considerably less than your present reading speed.

Nevertheless you haven't got the time to dwell on each word, so once you start, read determinedly and quickly. Read the words horizontally, left to right. For the test to tell us anything worthwhile, you must not glance back at the words nor refer to them until the conclusion of the test.

Memory and recall test

near	gasoline	brown	elephantine	queen
four	five	Picasso	Coca Cola	hand
finger	finger	Elizabeth	then	green
game	party	radio	under	hazy
age	white	nineteen	1901	war
era	Brussels	Diana	Oregon	likely
nail	Byzantine	Byzantium	elephant	elephantine
front	begun	princess	X-ray	vase

What happened during the fifteen seconds you allowed yourself to read those 40 words was that you recognised them and registered them in your short-term memory.

But because you were aware that it was a test requiring you to remember them, you concentrated and consciously transferred them into your permanent or long-term memory. If you are a normal person, that's where they are now.

So we know where they are, but can we dig them out? Can we recall them? Let's see.

1. Were there any numbers in the list and, if so, can you recall them?
2. What were the first three words?
3. What were the last three words?
4. Can you recall any of the colours listed?
5. There was a date. What was it?
6. A couple of personal names were in the list. Can you recall them?
7. An animal was mentioned. Can you name it?
8. Can you recall a part of the human body in the list?

Now you can check your attempt at recall with the list of words. It would be extraordinary if you remembered them all, but there are people with freakish memories who no doubt could reel them off, and in correct order, too.

The test demonstrates the difference between the functions of memory and recall. Given time, it is probable that you would be able to double the number of words you recalled as a response to the questions. Somehow, you just hadn't sent the right signals to release the information from your memory.

Association signals seem to be the key of good recall performance. It is likely that you successfully remembered *elephant*, *finger* (three repetitions, plus *hand* and *nail*), *Elizabeth* and *Diana* and *Picasso*. Possibly also *Byzantine* and *1901*. Familiar, long and striking words, names and numbers are more readily recalled than bland words like *under*, *then* and *begun*, to which you can attach few associations.

Can we not forget?

The 'three R's' of the memory process are **Registration**, **Retention** and **Recall**. We concluded in the earlier chapter on the mind and the memory that while there is little we can do about the retention element of the process, it is possible to improve registration and there are some tricks that will help our ability to recall.

When the memory process breaks down we call it 'forgetting'. Sometimes forgetfulness is momentary; at other times it is total, an unfathomable void. We are all familiar with 'memory blanks' and 'blind spots' – instances when no amount of deliberate memorising seems to help us recall the names of certain people, places or words. We're always bound to forget them. Why is this? We think it is because something interferes with the association pattern during the memory coding process – an ill-timed distraction, some emotional conflict – that distorts or even erases what ought to have been remembered. But these instances aside, most of the essentials of what we experience, see, hear, smell and read are locked up somewhere in our memories.

The best insurance for efficient recall is to concentrate and pay close attention to what you are reading; to be interested and involved in it, and to consciously make an agreement with yourself to remember it. To make doubly sure, you can re-read and revise; repetition is a proven device to assist remembering. For proof of this, spend another 15 seconds re-reading that list of 40 words. This time around you will remember many more of them.

Our ability to recall is, therefore, largely predetermined by how comprehensively we code material into our memories. Something read fleetingly, casually and for no purpose is unlikely to be retained and unlikely to be recalled. Yes, it is possible at times, with much determined effort and delay, to dredge up the remains of an insufficiently preserved memory (hypnosis has been known to extract subconsciously-observed car numberplates from the memories of people who, consciously, would have no hope of retrieving them) but, 'prevention is better than cure': record with care, recall at leisure.

The reading experience

There is a danger that with all this analysis you might be led to believe that reading is a complicated experience. It isn't, on the surface; for most of us it is an efficient means of learning and communicating, an exciting artform to send the senses reeling and the imagination soaring, and a pleasant way to relax and waste an hour or two.

But when we look into the structure of reading we find there is more to it than that. And as with any other activity, from swimming and tennis to playing chess and keeping healthy, if we wish to improve our performance we need to examine and upgrade the elements that make up the whole.

Many of these elements have already been pulled apart and poked at in previous chapters. What could be useful now is to look at them in the context of the reading experience.

We know, for example, about the roles of the eyes, the mind and the memory; about techniques to improve reading speed, understanding, retention and recall; about our own abilities, faults and potential. Now it's time to cement all this information into the form of the structure called *reading*.

Although we may not be conscious of it, a reading experience, even of the simplest kind, usually consists of four natural components: a *preview*, however momentary; the actual *reading*; a *postview*, which may amount to just a brief reflection on what has been read; and sometimes a *review*. In this chapter we will focus on each of these components and suggest how they might be fine-tuned to help us become even more efficient in our reading.

Reading and meaning

All reading material is not equal. Some is fascinating; a lot is boring and badly written. Some is reading we can't wait to feast our eyes on; sometimes it consists of texts so dense and dreary that we have to be dragged screaming to the page.

No matter; once we decide we want to or have to read a text we are committed, and we should then give it all we've got. To do otherwise is simply to throw away our time.

What we must learn to do is to psyche ourselves into a receptive, positive and even enthusiastic frame of mind before reading. This means understanding not only the purpose of our reading but its meaning, of which there are two kinds:

- Literal Meaning –   includes facts, information, news, names, dates, prices, etc.
- Inferential Meaning –   includes opinions, comment, argument, theory, rhetoric, etc.

The two are vastly different and make separate demands on the recognition and retention process. Those portions of the text carrying literal meaning require deliberate memorising, while inferential material requires us first to bring into play our previous knowledge and experience to decode it, and then to encode it into our memories. This is made possible by what is known as *schema* – a person's body of knowledge that provides the framework within which is placed the newly acquired knowledge. *Schema* allows it to be filed logically in the memory for easier recall.

Now, with the correct mind-set, we are ready to tackle a text.

The preview

It would be most unusual for anyone to start reading a slab of text without the remotest idea of what it was about. Invariably we have some clue – from the title or headline, from the name of the author, from the type of publication it is in. That is called a preview, and the purpose of it is to provide us with a sense of direction, a note of anticipation. Wheels and cogs whirr in our mind, neurones rearrange themselves, and in a split second we are prepared to receive information from this particular text and its subject.

We can use this natural instinct to improve our reading efficiency by going about it in a more structured, more considered way. There is sufficient proof that, like consulting a road map before driving through some foreign country, a thorough preview will make the reading journey easier and quicker.

Check the following to get some prior understanding of what you are about to read:

- The title or headline; chapter headings and sub-heads
- Summary of the work, or cover blurb
- Author's name, background and biography
- Author's previous work or books published
- Date of the work. Is it a revision, a reprint?
- List of contents, if there is one
- Flip through the pages. Watch for chapter headings, trigger words, illustrations, tables and so on to get a drift of the text
- Is it going to be a light read, or heavy going?
- Read the opening and closing paragraphs
- Will the text contribute to your knowledge or work?

Finally, in the light of what you've discovered, consider your reading strategy. How long will it take to read? Will you need to make notes? Are there sections you might safely ignore, or merely scan? What sections are going to require your close attention?

For a long article the preview might take you 20 seconds; for a book perhaps half a minute to a couple of minutes. And even though you may be anxious to start reading, those seconds you spend previewing could shave as many minutes off your reading time.

Now, like the anticipation aroused by the delicious aromas of a roast dinner wafting from the kitchen, you are razor-keen to start!

The reading

Gears are as necessary to reading as they are to a car. If there are texts that can be read at a uniform speed they must consist of the blandest, greyest, most insipid prose.

Most texts – a technical article, a description of a holiday location, a book, a newspaper editorial – contain highs and lows, turgid swamps and rocky terrain, all requiring a different approach and varying speeds. In short, flexibility. Some readers, familiar with a subject, might whizz through a section of fact-packed or technically demanding text which would stop another reader in his tracks. A lawyer capable of reading dense legalese at 550 w.p.m. might take an entire two-week holiday to finish a novel. The point here is to make allowances for variations in reading speed – even recognising in advance when you're required to change up or down a gear. Although the need to vary reading speed would appear to be self-evident, it is rarely recognised as a factor that can be helpful in increasing *overall* reading speed.

Reading speed

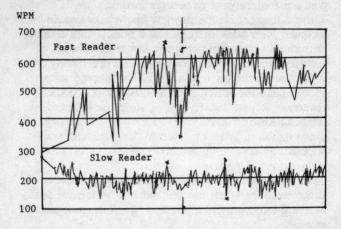

The graph above, for example, illustrates the reading speeds of two people; they're reading the same text over a period of about ten minutes. You will see that the trained fast reader has recorded a greater range of reading speeds than the slower reader. The reading behaviour of the fast reader looks to be extremely erratic, but there is real purpose in the highly-varied pattern. Let's compare the two for reading efficiency.

Slow Reader   Begins at about 270 w.p.m. but slows immediately and thereafter never exceeds 250 w.p.m. Average speed 195 w.p.m.

Fast Reader   Begins at 300 w.p.m. and soon gets into top gear, hitting and holding 600 w.p.m. for 3 minutes or so. Average speed 530 w.p.m.

For a crucial three minutes, the fast reader virtually skimmed over the text (which the slow reader found easy, too) even though the first three minutes averaged only about 350 w.p.m. In this example the fast reader was using an efficiency strategy: warming up enthusiastically, speeding where allowed, and once up to speed, maintaining an overall average. With training the slower reader could achieve a similar pattern.

So far we've placed the emphasis on speed, but the fluent reader will have assimilated the message of the text, if not all its details and texture, as well as the slow reader.

To do this it is necessary to follow a strict pattern of understanding: don't move on to the next sentence without understanding the previous one; don't move on to a fresh paragraph without understanding the paragraph before it. Keep your mind on the text all the time; keep satisfying yourself that you've got the point, you're following the argument, you're remembering the key facts.

To do this effectively you have to be critically receptive. This means clearing your mind of preconceptions and prejudices which can block the passage of new knowledge and ideas into your memory and slow the whole reading process.

It also means being alert to irrelevancies – unimportant passages, superfluous examples, anecdotes, repeated information, tangential comment – which you can skip through at speed.

Efficient readers are constantly on the lookout for certain signals in the text that can offer shortcuts to understanding such as italicized or bold passages, subheadings and summaries; and cue words and phrases:

> *Finally,* . . .
> *Therefore* . . .
> *In my opinion* . . .
> *In particular* . . .
> *Obviously* . . .

Words and expressions such as these are signals for

either more attention or less, and the ability to recognise them can contribute immeasurably to reading efficiency.

The postview

Again, this is an unconscious and natural component of the act of reading and can be developed to help improve comprehension.

When we finish reading a text there is almost always a momentary pause in which we reflect on what we have read. With a text that particularly interests or concerns us this reflection time might extend to many seconds. It is during these seconds of reflection that the content of the text attaches itself that much more deeply into our memories.

It follows, therefore, that we can deliberately use the reflection or postview function to reinforce our understanding and, by doing so, increase the likelihood of the essential message of the text being remembered.

In practice, we should weigh and consider the text in our minds. Do we have any questions? Does the text answer them? If not we should return to the relevant passage, or any sections of the text that gave us pause or difficulty.

A minute . . . a few minutes – but they could turn out to be the most valuable minutes in the entire reading experience.

The review

The review is a bolt-on component of the reading process but is pertinent to certain kinds of reading where extensive blocks of information have to be not only remembered but readily accessible.

There is one thing we know about reviewing (or revising as it is often called) and that is, the sooner it is undertaken after the original reading, the more effective it is.

In other words, if you read a text in the morning – say some learned essay, professional article, study course or technical notes – a review that same evening is more likely to commit a large part of it indelibly to memory than a review undertaken a week later.

The other important observation about reviewing is that it shouldn't be a slavish repetition of the original reading. It should take advantage of the fact that you are now familiar with the text and presumably have identified the key portions of it. This allows you to concentrate on the essential matter, to think about its meaning and especially to relate it to your present knowledge about that subject.

Information and learning are far too valuable to be thrown on to any old dump. Think of every text you read as a sort of building block you're using to construct your information bank. Efficient and conscientious reviewing will help cement the blocks more firmly in place.

- *As an exercise to reinforce the point, please review this chapter. You'll find in a test to be given later that your powers of memory and recall will have improved considerably since they were last tested.*

Scanning, skipping and skimming

Of this trio, skipping and skimming are more or less synonymous, and are the terms used to describe a type of reading akin to an owl's flight, covering a large area efficiently by hunting for and retrieving only what is needed. In the owl's case it is titbits like voles and fieldmice; in your case it is essential facts and arguments.

Scanning

Scanning, on the other hand, is a combing technique to extract specific information from a text – references to a certain subject or person, for example.

Suppose someone told you that last week *The Sunday Times* had published a story about a friend of yours who was clocked doing 120 m.p.h. by police on a motorway. Understandably, you are avid for the details. Now, you wouldn't look for this item by reading every word in the paper. Instead you would assume that the story would have a headline or an opening paragraph containing certain words like motorway, speed, police, 120 m.p.h. – and you would quickly leaf through the paper trying to spot them. Nine times out of ten you'd be reading the juicy details within half a minute as the result of your scanning.

Once you identify those 'trigger words' you believe will lead you to the required information, it's astonishing how you can make them almost jump from the page, just begging to be read. With some practice and concentration you can scan pages about as fast as you can turn them.

Scanning is *not* reading, and that's the important point. Your energies must be focused entirely on spotting those trigger words and specific references (like the owl's mouse) to the exclusion of everything else. It's a useful ability well worth developing.

Skimming

Skimming is a close relation to scanning but in this instance you cover the territory not so much like an owl after a single prey, but like a swallow, darting at great speed over a large area, sighting and devouring its diet of insects – in your case, significant words and ideas.

Skimming is a well recognised skill much used by professionals to cover a mass of reading material in a short time without missing its essentials. It is a skill that can only be honed on a solid foundation of efficient reading; a slow, inefficient reader would be wasting his or her time attempting to be a star skimmer!

If you have followed this book's instruction, advice and exercises so far, you will readily understand the function and technique of skimming. Like scanning, it is not the classic reading experience; it is a heightened state-of-mind activity requiring electric alertness and Hoover-like receptivity.

Expert scanning ability is not something that can be laboriously taught, but a discipline. However there are some points that might usefully be kept in mind.

- If the subject or text is strange to you, spend a short time on a preview; get a sense of what you should be looking for. Check any summaries or conclusions.
- Bring all your reading skills to bear in recognising signals like relevant names, facts and ideas. If you are familiar with the subject this process will be easy; if not, skim a little more cautiously.
- Watch for the emergence of thoughts and ideas; often you can skim through whole paragraphs of development before pausing to take in the anticipated conclusion.
- As far as eye travel is concerned, skimming places the emphasis on vertical, rather than

horizontal, movement. Be conscious of this: always force your eyes to skim downwards.

- While being alert to the peaks of a text – the parts you see or sense are significant – be equally alert to the verbal deserts: insignificant words, phrases, fillers, redundancies, entire paragraphs of greyness. Train yourself to fly over these.

Skimming is hardly worth its name if it can't pass over a text at something in excess of 1,000 w.p.m. or roughly three average book pages a minute.

That's the kind of speed you should aim for as a benchmark for your skimming ability – while still being able to give a fair and accurate account of the text you've skimmed.

Super reading

This leads us to the contentious area of 'super reading', the style of speed reading already referred to that supposedly gobbles up words at the rate of thousands of words a minute.

There may well be readers of this book who have this amazing ability, or the potential to develop it, and there is no reason why this should be discouraged. If a person can read at such a phenomenal speed, taking in all the essential information and enjoying the process, what's the harm? None at all, provided there is an awareness of the big difference between the utilitarian ability to scan and skim, and the art and craft of reading.

Final thoughts for the future

You'll have realised by now that reading is very much a multi-function experience. And it must have dawned long ago that efficient reading requires the co-ordination of many skills and areas of knowledge. We've touched on most of these in this book.

But there remains one area of learning that is indispensable to a proficient reader: *a better than average working vocabulary*. Without one you will be either tempted to skip over words you don't know (with the danger that you could be ignoring vital information), or be forever looking them up in a dictionary. A speed reader with a limited vocabulary is an oxymoron; you might want to look that up for a start.

The English language has over half a million words up for grabs. Some are in constant use; others are rarely seen. The average vocabulary is about 7,000 words while that of a well-read person might reach 15,000. At one end of the scale, nine out of ten telephone conversations in the US are conducted with a vocabulary of under 800 words; at the other, Shakespeare used over 20,000 words in his plays, and that was without the aid of dictionaries, which hadn't been invented then.

Nor is the language standing still. Dozens of new words enter it every day. Some graduate from slang, some are borrowed or stolen from other languages, some are invented to fill a need. Those are words, but for every new word coined hundreds of new *names* enter our lives – names of people, politicians, pop stars, newsmakers, book and film titles, new products. Efficient readers need to keep abreast of the times to keep their vocabularies up-to-date and in good working order.

Possessing a useful working vocabulary means not merely being able to recognise words but knowing their precise meanings: the meanings of for example, *empathy*, *decimate*, *burgeoning* and *paediatric*; and the differences between *parameter* and *perimeter*, *perennial* and *annual*, *flaunt* and *flout*, *lawful* and *legal*, and thousands of other confusing pairs.

There is no shortage of books and dictionaries that will help you boost your vocabulary, and two of them are in the *One Hour Wordpower* series:

- *Word Bank: Expanding Your Vocabulary* With a deceptively simple technique this book will help you add a thousand new, useful, apposite and elegant words to your everyday vocabulary. It's a book that's fun to use.
- *Word Check: Using Words Correctly* This is a concise handbook containing over 500 words often used incorrectly and others we're never quite sure about.

Where do you go from here?

Having come this far, and almost certainly having experienced real progress in your reading speed and levels of comprehension, are you going to leave it at that?

Unless you've decided that the goal of fulfilling your potential to read and remember efficiently is not for you, this would be a great pity. You know what to do, you know what you have to do; why not do it?

One way in which to extend the benefits of this book is to construct your own '28-Day Reading Programme'. Further exercises could be included here but why waste time with texts you don't need to read? A better idea is to use your everyday reading as practice material: newspaper and magazine articles (the longer the better), books (preferably non-fiction), background and study material associated with your work or interests.

Here are some tips on designing a programme that

should take you quite a way further in your quest for increased reading speed and efficiency.

A 28-day reading programme

1. Set aside at least 30 minutes a day specifically to read at speed, preferably at a time when you are not physically or mentally tired.
2. Select and measure out daily doses of reading, using the formula on page 66 to calculate the number of words. By now you should be practising with texts of between 2,000 and 6,000 words.
3. Time all your readings, record the times and calculate your w.p.m. rates using the formula on page 61.
4. Where applicable, use the previewing and postviewing technique.
5. On occasions, interrupt your faster-than-normal reading with a 2- or 3-minute sprint.
6. To test your comprehension, ask a member of your family, a friend or a colleague to ask you a series of questions on some of the texts.
7. Experiment with the various methods and techniques suggested in this book. Try to isolate those that seem to deliver the best results and concentrate on them.
8. After 14 days, draw up an assessment of your progress, using as a base the average speeds and comprehension levels recorded on your Progress Chart in this book.
9. If your progress is not up to expectations, try to analyse why. Are you really sure you've hit your limit?
10. Even though you may be disappointed, keep going for the second 14 days of the programme. You may be one of those for whom continual practice finally pays off.

And, finally . . . are you ready to recall?

This is the recall exercise promised at the end of the chapter on *The Reading Experience*. Assuming, as suggested, you dutifully reviewed that chapter after reading it, you should be confident that you can recall the essential facts in it.

Test No. 11

1. What are the four components of the reading experience? One of them is cited above.
2. How many types of meaning are there?
3. An unusual term was used to describe the body of knowledge we have that serves as the framework for newly acquired knowledge. What was it?
4. Which type of reader has a greater variation of reading speeds – the slow reader or the fast reader?
5. Would you say that it is true that the longer the period between the original reading and the reviewing or revising of it, the better it stays in the memory?
6. What sort of information has 'literal meaning'?
7. What are some of the things about a text that might quickly give us some clues about its content?
8. Is it true to say that in order to increase receptivity to a text, you should put yourself in the shoes of the author?

The answers to those eight questions will, of course, be found in that chapter, and six out of eight would be an acceptable score.

Speed tables, test answers and progress chart

Answers to comprehension tests

The answers to all the questions in the Comprehension Tests will of course be found in the test texts, but for convenience, here they are.

Test No. 1 (Page 14)

1. NO – the statement was 'as unknown as Outer Mongolia . . . and less accessible than Albania' 2. YES 3. NO – it was 200 million years ago 4. NO – it was half the world's chameleons. 5. NO – French 6. NO – it has doubled, not tripled 7. NO – larvae 8. YES 9. YES 10. NO – it is the indri lemur, not chameleon

Test No. 2 (Page 18)

1. NO – Toole, not O'Toole 2. NO – 1969 3. YES 4. YES 5. YES 6. YES 7. NO – Walker Percy 8. YES 9. NO – it was published posthumously 10. NO – in Mississippi State

Test No.3 (Page 20)

1. Bay of Naples 2. Parasites 3. (a) 4. (b) 5. (c)

Test No.4 (Page 35)

1. True 2. False 3. True 4. False 5. True 6. False 7. False 8. True 9. True 10. False

Test No.5 (Page 39)

1. False – it is the brain 2. True 3. True 4. False
5. False – it was *Paradise Lost* 6. True 7. The facts about
the epic journey were Spain/Columbus/1492/America

Test No. 6 (Page 66)

1. c 2. b 3. a 4. b 5. c 6. c 7. a 8. a 9. c 10. b

Test No. 9 (Page 83)

1. Donna Tartt 2. Any two of Henry, Bunny, Francis,
Charles, Camilla, Julian Morrow 3. Any of left-over
birthday cake, cream cheese and marmalade sandwiches,
maraschino cherries 4. Richard Papen 5. Vermont
6. Henry 7. *The Secret History* 8. Pizza Hut 9. Yes
10. Bunny

Test No. 10 (Page 86)

1. Yes, Cheshire 2. A child's fist 3. Holland
4. Parmesan 5. Afternoon 6. Brie 7. Yes 8. Decaying
carcasses or game 9. Knocked out flies 10. Marble

Speed Tables

To find your reading speed in w.p.m., read off your reading time (in seconds, i.e. 2 min 20 sec is 2 × 60 = 120 + 20 = 140 sec) under the appropriate Exercise.

	TEST 2		TEST 3		TEST 4
sec	w.p.m.	sec	w.p.m.	sec	w.p.m.
210	250	50	235	40	258
200	260	45	265	39	264
190	275	42	280	38	270
180	290	40	295	37	279
170	310	38	310	36	286
160	330	35	340	35	295
150	350	32	370	32	320
140	375	30	395	30	344
130	400	29	410	27	382
120	440	28	420	25	412
110	480	26	455	24	430
100	525	24	490	22	470
90	580	22	540	20	515
80	655	20	590	18	575
75	700	18	670	16	645
70	750	15	790	14	740
65	810	12	980	12	860
60	875	10	1180	10	1032
55	950				
50	1050				

TEST 5		TEST 6		TEST 7	
sec	w.p.m.	sec	w.p.m.	sec	w.p.m.
120	216	150	220	65	215
115	225	140	240	55	235
110	236	130	250	50	260
105	247	120	275	45	285
100	260	110	300	42	310
95	273	100	330	40	320
90	288	90	370	38	340
85	305	85	390	36	360
80	324	80	410	34	380
75	345	75	440	32	400
70	370	70	470	30	430
65	400	65	510	28	460
60	430	60	550	26	495
55	470	55	600	24	535
50	520	50	660	22	585
45	580	45	730	20	645
40	650	40	830	18	715
35	750	35	950	16	805
30	850	30	1100	14	920
				12	1080

TEST 8		TEST 9		TEST 10	
sec	w.p.m.	sec	w.p.m.	sec	w.p.m.
55	230	180	210	160	230
50	260	170	225	150	245
45	285	160	240	140	260
42	310	150	255	130	280
40	320	140	275	120	300
38	340	130	295	110	330
36	360	120	320	100	365
34	380	110	350	90	400
32	400	100	385	85	430
30	430	90	425	80	460
28	460	85	450	75	490
26	495	80	480	70	520
24	535	75	510	65	560
22	585	70	550	60	600
20	645	65	590	55	660
18	715	60	640	50	730
16	800	55	700	45	800
14	920	50	770	40	900
12	1080	45	850	35	1050
		40	960		
		35	1100		

Progress chart – Reading speed and comprehension

Date	Exercise	Speed w.p.m.	Comp %
	Test 1 Reading and comprehension		
	Test 2 Reading and comprehension		
	Test 3 Reading and comprehension		
	Test 4 Comprehension		
	Test 5 Comprehension		
	Test 4 Reading		
	Test 5 Reading		
	Test 6 Reading and comprehension		
	Test 7 Reading		
	Test 8 Reading		
	Test 9 Reading and comprehension		
	Test 10 Reading and comprehension		
	Test 11 Recall		
	Averages		